Inventing Education

Inventing Education

Georgetown Students and D.C. Youth Learn From Each Other

by John C. Hirsh

With a Foreword by Robert Emmett Curran
a Chapter by Bradley Galvin
and Photographs by Harry Mattison

NEW ACADEMIA PUBLISHING

Washington, DC

Library of Congress Control Number: 2022909338
ISBN 979-8-9852214-3-5 paperback (alk. paper)

New Academia Publishing, 4401-A Connecticut Ave. NW, #236, Washington, DC 20008
info@newacademia.com - www.newacademia.com

By the same author:

POWER AND PROBITY IN A DC COOPERATIVE: The Life and Death of Sursum Corda

VYGOTSKY'S CHILDREN: Georgetown and Oxbridge Students Meet Urban Youth

MEDIEVAL LYRIC: Middle English Lyrics, Ballads and Carols

CHAUCER AND THE CANTERBURY TALES: A Short Introduction

NAPOLEON: ONE IMAGE, TEN MIRRORS. Essays edited with Roberto Severino

THE BOUNDARIES OF FAITH: The Development and Transmission of Medieval Spirituality

SURSUM CORDA: Teaching Urban Youth to Read

THE REVELATIONS OF MARGERY KEMPE: Paramystical Practices in Late Medieval England

HOPE EMILY ALLEN: Medieval Scholarship and Feminism

BARLAM AND IOSAPHAT: A Middle English Life of Buddha

WESTERN MANUSCRIPTS OF THE TWELFTH THROUGH THE SIXTEENTH CENTURY IN LEHIGH UNIVERSITY LIBRARIES: A Guide to the Exhibition

Contents

Dedication

Unsurprisingly but very warmly I dedicate this book to all who have taken part with me in the tutoring and literacy program that has flourished for more than thirty years among Georgetown University, Sursum Corda, and Golden Rule Apartments, whether as student tutors, student learners, parents, care givers, residents, university or apartment administrators, and anyone who welcomed or supported us at all.

I salute tutors and learners especially, for the comradeship that comes from a shared enterprise rooted in mutual belief, and for the age appropriate friendships that grew up among them, as they acknowledged and sought to address the evident inequalities and injustices our nation has allowed, even as they both taught and learned from each other.

Acting together, and over many years, tutors and learners embraced both difference and collegiality, and sought to find in their associations the beginnings of a better future for us all.

J. C. H.

In the deserts of the heart
Let the healing fountain start,
In the prison of his days
Teach the free man how to praise.

W. H. Auden.

Foreword

by Robert Emmett Curran,
author of *A History of Georgetown University* (2010)

One of the most significant changes of the 1960s was that of the relationship of urban universities with their local communities. As part of President Lyndon Johnson's commitment to building a "Great Society," Title I of the Higher Education Act of 1965 authorized funding for community service by institutions of higher education. Georgetown University, largely through the prodding of student activists, had already begun to respond to the growing awareness of the inequity and lack of opportunity confronting Washington's now majority Black community. Under the umbrella of the Georgetown University Community Action Program (GUCAP), by the mid-Sixties more than 800 students were involved in everything from tutoring inner city children to lobbying for civil rights legislation. The tutorial program at Sursum Corda was a natural outgrowth of this development. Sursum Corda, a town house complex in northwest Washington, a few blocks from the Capitol, had been built by private funding as well as subsidies from the Department of Housing and Urban Development. The private financing had come from Georgetown alumni, so it was natural that the 199-unit facility became, in 1969, the site of a tutoring program run by Georgetown students.

A year after Sursum Corda opened, John Hirsh joined the English Department faculty. Hirsh had the singular accomplishment of not only teaching in two very distinctive fields, that of Medieval as well as American studies, but of becoming a prolific publisher in them, particularly on Medieval topics. He also served, for many years, as the virtual university secretary for the selection and preparation of candidates for the ultra-competitive Marshall scholarships, of which there were more than a few Georgetown recipients during his watch. But it was the outreach program at Sursum Corda, of which he became the director in 1989, in which over the next 27 years he was to make, arguably, his most important contributions to Georgetown, as well as to the larger community of which it was a part.

In 2017 Hirsh published *Power and Probity in a DC Cooperative: The Life and Death of Sursum Corda* (Washington, D.C.: New Academia Publishing). *Inventing Education*, as the reader will quickly discover, is also about the housing cooperative on First Place, inasmuch as it framed and very much impacted and shaped decisions about the tutoring program that Hirsh headed. The focus of the present volume is the program itself -- its evolution, the difficulties it encountered, the successes it realized – but Sursum Corda is an overshadowing presence in its pages. Inventing Education, as Hirsh points out at the outset, is a recollection of instruction very much within the context of the community and the city in which it took place.

As Hirsh notes, the program through its first two decades had been essentially a service operation, in which Georgetown students served as unsupervised homework aides to youngsters at Sursum Corda. Hirsh early on determined that the operation had to be radically reconstructed, if it were to be of any educational worth. The informal homework assistance, under his direction, quickly mutated into the formal teaching of literacy to these young residents. In brief, the new focus aimed at introducing the student-residents to the world of books, to the incredible knowledge that was accessible to those who can read. That meant preparing the student-tutors to have the skills to lead the young learners into reading, including comprehending the texts that reading was opening to them. In a program whose tutors had historically had a high turnover rate, as volunteer operations tend to produce, Hirsh was able to retain tutors beyond one or two semesters. That proved to be a vital factor in the success that the program came to enjoy.

That long-term achievement points to one of the remarkable elements of Hirsh's relationship to the program: his status as advisor. This was a period, one needs to recall, in which faculty advisors to student organizations were becoming purely nominal. In that climate it is remarkable that Hirsh remained more of a traditional advisor, more manager or director of the program, than advisor in name only. Part of his ability to retain a more traditional status in the Sursum Corda program may well have been his own heavy involvement in the front lines. Each semester without fail, Hirsh was responsible for the reading development of a particular Sursum Corda participant. Hirsh was experiencing the program just as any Georgetown undergrad would have. That immersion may well have provided him the common ground with student tutors that enabled him to direct, a bond that academic credentials alone could not create.

Hirsh leads us through the uneven evolution of the program, from its initial use of phonics as its chief mode of getting learners to confront words and to build from there, to more complex and rewarding methods. Through Hirsh's own pursuit of literacy pedagogy, including several summers at the University of California, Berkeley, the "whole language" approach toward the teaching of reading became the major influence in constructing a methodology for the program. Whole language teaching involves getting the reader to encounter the meaning of life through words; of utilizing writing to develop the student's reading proficiency; of building trust between tutor and learner, if the latter is to gain confidence and ability in reading. The goal was to promote reflection, on the student's part, and to stimulate his imagination in engaging the text. From the strategic use of familiar objects and situations the learners well knew, they were encouraged to explore the world they did not yet know, all in the service of personal growth, both for the learner as well as for the tutor. That led to the tutors keeping logs. Such inventories of their students' reading experience, in Hirsh's judgement, were far better evaluations of students' development than standard quantitative measurements, such as test scores.

Through the effective use of what he calls gobbets, or vignettes, Hirsh brings the community of Sursum Corda viscerally alive. Although professing a non-didactic approach in recounting his pedagogical experience of nearly three decades, storytelling serves as a way of instruction. He communicates all too well the effect that a drug-pervasive community had on its children and their ability to learn, or even to want to learn. He describes the impact that involvement with the program had upon the tutors.

On the rare occasion he suspends his non-didactic stance to impose a pithy lesson, such as his putdown of the "easy belief that since interaction [between Blacks and Whites] infects, the best thing that White people can do is to tend their own exotic gardens, or else they will make a cultural wasteland of everything." Or this blunt observation: "Tutors can open doors, but not shut them, and probably shouldn't try." Or this wise reflection on delivering some core truths to two young Sursum Corda boys about drugs: "I hoped, I somewhat believed, that perhaps in later time what was once said by one who cared for them might resonate, and leave a weight, if only that of a feather, on the right side of the scales. And . . . so that, little as I like sanctimony, I did not hesitate to have my say."

Sursum Corda, while certainly the longest-lasting, was but one of five reading programs with which Hirsh has been involved in Washington, D.C. and London, Great Britain. For over a half century, Hirsh has had a connection, as both student and faculty member, with Oxford University. As a visiting fellow at Pembroke College at Oxford in 1992-93, Hirsh wanted to explore reading pedagogy in inner city London. Chapter 4, "New Britain," traces his experience of working at an elementary school with Bangladeshi students from the Tower Hamlet's district of London. Unlike his D.C. students, these were older, multi-lingual, and in a multi-racial school environment, with English and Bangladeshi students in one classroom, a challenge that Sursum Corda did not present. Nonetheless, Hirsh found common ground in both places as well as common lessons. The chief one: "Whatever the learner's age, the teacher is in some way seeking to empower, not to mainstream, the student . . ." His central goal is to enable the student, if not to flourish, at least to make his way in a society that can in many ways be alien.

A 2017 report published by the British Equality and Human Rights commission, *Healing a Divided Britain: The Need for a Comprehensive Race Equality Strategy* gave Hirsh a better purchase on the symbiotic relationship between economic/social justice and education. The latter, lacking the undergirding of the former, will "be at a loss," as he succinctly puts it, to prepare children for life's business.

Hirsh concludes that "education is a mystery, and we move among forces we understand only in part." Hirsh's journey, both at the university levels of Georgetown and Oxford, as well as at the elementary levels of Sursum Corda and Towers Hamlet, has been one in which understanding, slowly and unevenly, penetrates mystery, never coming close to exhausting it, for sure, but by utilizing methods validated by experience, advances and broadens learning. All in the service of bringing education ever closer to its democratic ideal. For that excellent reason does Hirsh aver that "my recollection leaves me nothing to regret."

This is a journey that should deeply interest not only those in the field of literacy pedagogy but anyone concerned about the role of education in building, brick by brick, a more equitable society.

Acknowledgments

After thirty-two years of working in two always rewarding if sometimes challenging programs, a list of everyone who has assisted or supported us would fill a book as long as this one, and I must ask that the Dedication be allowed to testify to my gratitude to many who have helped.

But it is important to acknowledge and thank those at Sursum Corda and at Golden Rule Apartments who have welcomed, supported and assisted us over the years.

Georgetown began sending students to work at Sursum Corda in 1970, but by the end of the 1980's it had shrunk in size, and was operating as a homework program, with only limited instruction of the students who took part. In 1989 however, the Dean of Students, John J. DeGioia, now President of the university, resolved to reform these practices, and in due course the program advanced to one which instructed students in what they might accomplish and how they might do so, while preserving a close but overseen relationship between tutor and learner alike as an essential part of the program. This new program was aided by many a one, but without the late Ms. Allene Harper, our Community Coordinator, and Ms. Christine Nicholson, the Resident Manager at Sursum Corda, who together welcomed and guided us for 27 years, and without Sister Diane Roche, R.S.C.J., and Ms. Alverta Munlyn, who guided Sursum Corda itself during the same period, our work would have been far less effective, joyful, and satisfying than it became.

The transition of the program from Sursum Corda to Golden Rule Apartments, necessitated by the destruction of Sursum Corda in 2017, was suggested by Mr. Shiv Newaldass, a former Sursum Corda resident, who then initiated contacts with colleagues at Mission First of Philadelphia in order to help bring it about. The process was further expedited by Officer Darrin Bates of the MPD, another former Sursum Corda resident, who assisted invaluably with a myriad of practical details. At Georgetown particular thanks go to Professor Ricardo Ortiz, former Chair of the English Department, who both encouraged the transition to Golden Rule, and secured its institutional support; to Professor Randall Bass, Vice President for Strategic Education Initiatives, for his assistance, both financial and academic, in what was to come; and to Dr. Andrea Wisler, Executive Director of the Center for Social Justice at Georgetown, who proved a model of encouragement, insight and practical support. At Golden Rule Apartments we were greeted and supported during our first three years by Mr. Patrick Williams, who made the transition smooth and welcoming, and by his assistant, Ms. Ania Hendy, who spoke with evident understanding to tutors and learners alike. In the first year of the pandemic we had the good fortune to work with Mr. William Foster, then subsequently with Mr. Frederick Hawkins, who were of the greatest of help in connecting with our learners and their families.

To all of these, as to many others, tutors and learners alike tender our best thanks for helping us in very many ways. In July 2019 I read no. 10, "Song," and no. 13, "How Not to Celebrate Christmas," both from chapter 3, to a work-in-progress seminar at Campion Hall, Oxford, and I am most grateful for the interest and the comment they occasioned. I am further grateful to Ms. Mary Ellen Connell, a friend and neighbor, and to my sister, Ms. Margo Kelly, both of whom read this book and made helpful and perceptive suggestions. Ms. Paula Farina, an accomplished teacher of young children,

both proofread the book professionally and offered many helpful editorial suggestions with her usual sympathy, insight and understanding. Dr. Anna Lawton, New Academia's founder and Publisher, was of great help in seeing the book through the press.
J. C. H.

Chapter 1

Another Beginning

Introduction

This is the book I would have liked to have read before I began working, first as faculty advisor, then effectively as director, of a teaching program in which Georgetown University undergraduates worked, for the most part one-on-one, with a group of about twenty-five bright kindergarten to sixth grade (K-6) children who lived in an urban community in Washington, D.C. known as Sursum Corda. What follows is a short record of that program, together with some accounts of a like program at nearby Golden Rule Apartments that followed the Sursum Corda model and began in September 2017, soon after the April 2017 close of the program at Sursum Corda. It also includes an account, in chapter four, of some related work I did in an urban school in London. Overall, it is an account, warts and all, of challenges and problems, as well as apparent and occasional successes we met with in Washington, of missteps and lucky guesses. Although it is not in any sense a "Handbook" intended to show how to establish, conduct, or expand such programs, I hope that it will interest anyone in a similar position, perhaps helping to anticipate problems, or to recognize difficulties as they arise -- if only by seeing that we have been there, too. It offers no prescriptions, but it may inform inductively, even though no two programs are the same, and any program will adjust its practices over time according to circumstances, just as we did.

The book thus contains a recollection of our program, not only its history, but also a consideration of some of the issues that confront such programs generally. It also draws upon one other program in Washington and three in London with which I have been connected. But I will usually refer to the program that Georgetown University sponsored in Sursum Corda for forty-seven years, which I effectively oversaw for the last twenty-seven.

The name Sursum Corda means "Lift Up Your Heart" in Latin and occurs in the Preface of the Roman Catholic Latin mass. According to Dom Gregory Dix, a scholar of such things, it may have been incorporated into the mass as early as 150 A.D.; it continues in use today. The community that bore that name came to an end in the spring of 2018, when the residents, some of whom had lived there since the community was founded in 1970, were effectively forced from their homes by developers. The following November, the community was demolished. One can learn more about this long, painful process in my book, *Power and Probity in a D.C. Cooperative: The Life and Death of Sursum Corda* (2018).

The focus of this book is on the possibilities cross-cultural neophyte education holds out, particularly as it relates to the ways in which advantaged, usually middle-class students address less advantaged urban children, whom they otherwise would have been most unlikely to know well, if at all. The *New York Times* columnist David Brooks has several times pointed to a sense of fear and mutual distrust, born from a lack of meaningful connection, that is rampant among us, and seems to have grown, not diminished, in recent years. Though we were largely concerned with the language arts in general and with reading in particular, the Sursum Corda Program maintained two characteristics that were far from universal among such programs, the second of which is markedly relevant to these concerns. First, an engagement between tutor and learner that offered a degree of autonomy to the Georgetown undergraduates who took part in it, but which was – or at least became – an informed autonomy of the sort that used to be universal among teachers, but is being undercut by certain scripted programs that operate as much in the interest of quantitative measurement as of children. As our program developed, our tutors met regularly apart from their tutorials, discussed what they were doing with their learners, and came to understand together, from me, and from books, how they might improve their practice.

The second, and no less important, hallmark of the program concerned the relationship between tutor and learner. As the program developed over the years, it instituted a policy of two hour-long meetings a week between tutor and learner, on Tuesday and Thursday nights from 7 to 8pm, supplemented by a third on-campus seminar that took place on Wednesday afternoon or evening, between the tutors and me, without the children being present. Occasionally, particularly in the early days, these would be supplemented by a Saturday excursion, in which some or all of the tutors would take a number of children on an excursion – to the zoo, to play basketball in the Georgetown gym, to a movie – which had the effect of deepening the relationships of tutor and student. This relationship was central, but relatively uncomplicated, except when it was not. It had to take into account legal constraints, as well as sensitivity to gender, age disparities (the least complicated, as it turned out), and race. But throughout the twenty-seven years I was associated with the program, our concern for the safety of the children was unrelenting and paramount, always and everywhere. The fact that we prized the relationship between student and learner as highly as we did made attention to the physical circumstances of the relationship the first order of business. Our invariable practice was never to allow a single tutor to be alone with a single learner, even when, as often happened, the tutor became well known to the learner's family and was accepted and trusted by them. Oversight by others was a part of our practice. This might include fellow tutors, when a small group of tutors and learners went to the movies, to a museum, or to a basketball game together. These excursions required my agreement, consent of the parent or caregiver, and subsequent discussion of the trip in the van ride to Sursum the following week, in our Wednesday seminar, or both.

We took the trouble we did because the relationships that emerged mattered for our practice. For the most part, Georgetown tutors not only knew what they were about pedagogically, they also, within certain agreed upon limitations, knew their learners -- and often their learners' families, too. Without this circumstance, the learning could have become perfunctory, and only one-way. But Sursum Corda tutors learned as much as they taught, even when they felt hard pressed to say precisely what it was that they now understood.

The social and economic circumstances between tutor and learner often differed greatly, and what one learned was not often a lesson for the other. But even when, as sometimes happened, learner and tutor never really bonded, what finally mattered was what each one came to assume. Thus, what had been learned was sometimes unlearned, an attitude toward race fed by the media, or by fake history. Very many students entered the program informed by a kind of American apartheid, in which race and class were only rarely broached.

It is worth mentioning that much of what we undertook could be seen as a part of certain teachings long present in Catholic social thought. But when such issues presented themselves, I would sometimes quote Hillel's three questions:
- If I am not for myself, who will be for me?
- If I am only for myself, then what am I?
- and If not now, when?

It was clear to many of my Georgetown students, as it was to me, that our work did not lack a religious dimension, even if it was one we explored only too rarely in class. But for the last few years, I assigned both Pope Benedict's encyclical *God Is Love* (available online at vatican.va), and Peter Edelman's

So Rich, So Poor: Why It's So Hard to End Poverty in America (2012) to our Wednesday seminar, not only in order to suggest a deeper goal for our program than a well-run state, but also to acknowledge the need for civic virtue too.

Thirty years ago, in the early days of my involvement with the program, the only opposition we encountered came from the left. The objection was not that our tutors were uninstructed in their craft, which could have been argued at the time, but that such racial and cultural attitudes as they had developed over the years were not to the advantage of the children whom they were about to teach. It seemed, at the time, not an entirely unreasonable objection, particularly for those who had never engaged in such work, but as time would tell, it was simply mistaken. The children were – or at least became – unwitting teachers of their tutors on issues never discussed, and when that happened, the tutors never listened more attentively. Assumptions vanished in the face of a face, and what became central to our program was not only a degree of sometimes imperfect instruction (to which I will return), but also a shared and negotiated experience in meeting people who, for reasons of age, race, or gender, are unlike ourselves. And getting to like them. And reading and, in due course, discussing books together.

These two hallmarks – freedom to engage in teaching the Language Arts with a certain degree of competence, and a measured relationship between tutor and learner – are not universal in such programs, in Georgetown or elsewhere. For a number of years, I was a member of the International Reading Association (the IRA), an excellent, international (if substantially American, in my experience) professional body for K-12 teachers, and I attended several of its national meetings.

It was in this context that I heard an interesting paper from a teacher at a Middle School who had recently founded a program that drew in high school students to teach his primary school charges. My recollection is that the same older students did not appear every time, and though the practice was conducted weekly and one-on-one, attendance could be irregular; faces changed regularly. The teaching, however, did not. In what may well have been appropriate to the circumstances, the tutors were directed what to teach, and how to do so: phonics figured importantly, as did repeated reading. It seemed to me a good effort. I noted our shared use of the excellent practice of repeated reading, and I saw too why we had begun as we had. The Georgetown students who took part in our program wished well to those whom they instructed, but proceeded without much attention to cultural difference.

In such circumstances, age differences can work as a positive advantage, allowing a degree of personal openness on both sides. I have already noted that what all students, older and younger, learn in such cases often speaks effectively to unacknowledged assumptions, but the setting for this acquisition is rarely forgotten. Whenever I have met a former tutor, his or her first question is usually to inquire after a former learner. Unfortunately, we were only very rarely able to keep up with our learners more than a year or two after they left our program, with the result that we could hardly ever track them, or our outcomes, for very long at all. But we were always very glad to hear, as we did through the grapevine more times than I can remember during the years in which the program rolled on, that another of our learners had gone to college, or landed a good job, or otherwise distinguished himself or herself. However, the frequency with which families moved in and out of the community, or children left home, or tutors graduated, among other reasons, always prevented anything like a full accounting.

Thus, I very much meant it when I said that this book is not a how-to-do-it guidebook, but is instead a record of instruction, one that concerns itself with how we operated in practice, and why such pedagogy as we offered is best not separated from the circumstances and the community in which it takes place. What follows is a description not only of the place where we worked and what we did there, but also a recounting of the social and personal difficulties that learners and tutors confronted, whether together or separately. Tutors quickly understood that their work had implications beyond the moment and could help to make connections that otherwise might not come about.

Although I have named here, with actual or implied thanks, those who were good enough to support and assist us in the early years of our program and later, I have avoided naming individual tutors, or saying what it was I believed any one of them finally learned. Tutoring is, like teaching, an individual occupation, and any such conclusion is their property, not mine, who would probably get it wrong were I so foolish as to try to describe it. But it was the tutors, the children, and the parents and caregivers, together with those in the community who had our back, that sustained the Sursum Corda program, as others now do at Golden Rule, and it is to them that the book is dedicated.

By now I hope that it can be said without too much contradiction that the great victories in Voting Rights and Civil Rights should not only continue, but also allow for other more complicated efforts, addressing issues of age, race, gender, and culture, as we sought, however indirectly, to do. It was our belief that education, and specifically the ability to read critically and to write well, was at the heart of that effort, and that was why they were also at the heart of our program.

When, in September 1989, I began working with a tutoring program Georgetown University had been supporting for young, K-6 children at an apartment complex in North West Washington called Sursum Corda, I believed that whatever else happened, our teaching would almost certainly be remedial. But as our program grew, I came to understand that intervention by a group of able, committed, and eventually informed undergraduates who engage the children as active readers and co-participants has advantages that cannot be called remedial. As September turned into November, we began to change what we had been doing, a process that would never really end. The summer before, I had gone to the University of California at Berkeley and taken two graduate courses in the School of Education there, one on teaching reading to children with reading difficulties, the other on the assessment and evaluation of such children. It was these courses, responding to certain questions we had been forced to confront concerning our practices, that helped us to rethink our program, and to effectively begin again.

Georgetown students had been working at the community of Sursum Corda since 1970, almost as soon as it opened, but during the 1980s, a combination of internal administrative difficulties and a suddenly active drug trade had combined to limit the usefulness of all of the programs there, ours included. Sursum Corda, until it was levelled in 2017 in the dubious interests of urban development, was a low-rise HUD-subsidized housing complex of 199 units, covering 4.6 acres of ground (extending to over 5 acres if you count sidewalks and streets), and bounded by North Capitol and First Street NW on two sides, K and M Streets NW on the other two. Constructed by private and public funds between 1968 and 1969, the contract for its construction had been put out to tender, with the result that instead of the usual high-rises, the project was designed as town houses, most containing three, four, or five bedrooms, specifically intended for families. There were also some with one bedroom, and some studios.

It had from its beginning the reputation for being a difficult place: tenants often acted, individually or together, according to their own lights, and did not easily take direction from outsiders, including the owner, a dedicated and well-intentioned Catholic, who had certain well-formulated ideas as to what constituted appropriate behavior. Supporting the early owner was a group of concerned businessmen and friends, several of them either Georgetown graduates or having Georgetown connections, who secured and provided federal funding, thanks in no small part to Senator Robert Kennedy of New York, for the units and a related community center to be built. A Residents' Association was also established that entered into frequent dialogue with the owner as to what practices should be encouraged and observed. When management proved difficult over the first decade, the owner sold the property. However, a change in the tax law meant that the new owners could no longer claim certain tax advantages, so they introduced a number of practices and requirements intended to address issues of order and compliance, requirements that those who lived there thought were detrimental to their sense of community. So the Residents' Association sprang into action, and in 1987 initiated a rent strike that effected another change of management.

A 1992 HUD grant allowed the Association to acquire the property themselves, and thus to become a cooperative, a designation that remained in effect until the end. Under an agreement with the Tenants Association, Georgetown University was able to operate a homework program for the children, and it was to the Tenants Association that our changed program was finally responsible. The arrangement was at once informal and friendly, but our daily associations were with others who worked and usually lived there, primarily with Ms. Allene Harper, the first Sursum Corda coordinator who, employed at a modest salary by Georgetown, announced our program to the residents, signed up the children whose parents asked her to do so, and developed good relationships with our tutors as well as with the residents generally. As what we asked of the children became known, we had in fact to refuse admission to very few of those who applied, and could in most cases promise admission in due course (that is, next semester or the one after) to almost everyone. We were also very helpfully supported and assisted by those of the parents and Sursum Corda officials whom we came to know well: Ms. Christine Nicholson, who later came to take Allene's place; Ms. Alverta Munlyn, at the time Vice President of the Resident's Association; and very much by Sister Diane Roche, RCSJ, then the Resident Manager of Sursum Corda, who oversaw the property when we began to reconstitute the program in 1989, and who supported us, as she did the community, throughout.

In the very early history of our program, before our 1989 revision, a small number of Georgetown students would travel weekly to Sursum Corda in order to help the children who lived there with their homework. In those years, as one of the tutors subsequently wrote to me, the number of student tutors who went weekly could fit comfortably in a single car, and their work depended on the homework assignments the children brought with them. In keeping with its practice, the university was not then involved in what or how the students taught. The idea seemed to be that the students should learn by doing, but what they did was up to them, and it was naively expected that the children involved would somehow benefit from the association.

Under these circumstances, there was never any question of giving academic credit to the student tutors involved, but in 1988, as our revision was progressing, I wondered about that policy, and in due course proposed a course for tutors who took part in our program. I was deflected deftly by an associate dean who suggested that the idea simply needed more study: he had no difficulty in allowing credit for our tutors, he insisted, but had some doubts about other groups within the academic community, and was still considering how to differentiate. The drama people had been after him as well, and though he was willing, of course, to allow credit for whomever, as it were, played Hamlet, he was less willing to do so for everyone who carried a spear in the last act, and so on. It seemed reasonable, and I reluctantly agreed that we should "make haste slowly," or *festina lente* as the Latin has it, a commonplace term that became the first, if soon abandoned, motto of the program.

Not long afterwards, I talked with a woman who had grown up in a disadvantaged community, one in which college students tutored, receiving academic credit. Her experience had been mixed. The undergraduates were intelligent and engaging. They did what they were supposed to, helped with homework, and were fun to have around, though she never got to know any of them very well. But when the semester finished, so were they. When I asked how she and her friends felt about this development, she said frankly that since they hardly knew their tutors, the damage was small. They had at first thought of the tutors as potential friends, but then reckoned they had been mistaken. But she did not actually call for a relationship of many years, such as had existed at Sursum Corda in the past; instead, she thought that it was more important that the terms and the details of the engagement should be known generally. Children change and develop more quickly than college students, she pointed out, and a change of tutor is not necessarily a bad thing, particularly if it is expected.

But the problem of relationships can be complex, since, like their learners, undergraduate students are in some ways not masters of their fate, and often for good reason cannot continue beyond a semester even when they want to do so. This was a problem that, for us at least, became perennial.

In the end, we had to be very sure that everyone knew the constraints of the program once we began to award credit, a circumstance that made direction easier. But the learners, young as they were, came to understand the rules, and sometimes, individual children seemed rather to welcome a change of tutor as he or she moved from childhood into youth.

And now it is February of 2019 and, after the demise of Sursum Corda, I am directing a new, similar program at Golden Rule Apartments, only a few blocks from where Sursum Corda once stood. I am considering the twelve Georgetown students who are now our tutors. It is the second semester of our second year here, and though our work at Golden Rule is in some ways a continuation of our work at Sursum Corda, the program is, for now at least, smaller and, like the children, better sheltered, with the result that our academic outcomes are at least as positive. Already patterns are beginning to emerge. Six of the twelve tutors now with us have returned from last semester, when we had a total of ten in our still-developing program. Only three had initially signed up to continue, but as happened last year, when the moment came, they did what they had to do, and returned to their young learners, who in two cases had asked them to return. But these programs respond necessarily to changes in academic practices, and even Sursum Corda's last semester was subject to the strictures of major requirements, with the result that some tutors simply could not repeat their commitment.

It is still early days at Golden Rule as I am writing, where we were warmly welcomed and perceptively informed by Mr. Patrick Williams, the Residential Service Manager. My impression is that a change of tutor will be less difficult here – perhaps harder on the tutor than the learner – where the children are more closely watched and know it. But I have noticed that I no longer react to a tutor's necessarily abbreviated commitment as I once did (with somewhat exaggerated regret), even though I still remember what happened toward the end of my first or perhaps second year at Sursum: both parents of one young man made a point of thanking their son's now graduating tutor for the four years she had voluntarily supported and assisted their son, raising his report card grades from C's and D's to A's and B's, they said.

My experience has been that our program needed to be rethought at reasonable but regular intervals, and thus it was that in 1989, responsible parties considered that although the program had carried on for almost twenty years, it had somewhat faded, in spite of some residual student interest. A very able student director spent some days before her graduation writing a letter to the powers that be, detailing its several imperfections, only to find herself called in by said powers and asked why she had allowed things to descend to such a state. But she may have had a greater effect than we then knew (knowing my sympathies, she had confided in me). A general announcement subsequently went forth calling for interested volunteers, and a surprising number came. Because I had alerted the then Dean of Students (now President of the university) to my interest, I was included. Still, old ways die hard. From the first, the idea was that the university should not get too deeply involved (there was then no credit involved in any work the students undertook), and that the program should be handed over to the students as soon as was practicable.

We found what I have already alluded to: an irregular and diminished homework program that brought tutor and child together in difficult circumstances. The tutor's role was usually to produce right answers, so that the child would get a check mark in the teacher's grade book the next day. It was not that we were against homework, we told ourselves, (though knowing the very reasonable English practice of not assigning it in early grades, I personally was), but that the children viewed homework as such a chore that any active engagement with learning had to begin elsewhere. Thanks to some felt advice we received from a recently retired primary school teacher, we began by seeking to teach the student tutors some of the rudiments of phonics, with the idea that we would use workbooks to give direction to our time together. In the beginning this approach seemed helpful: it was not difficult to teach Georgetown tutors how to employ elementary instruction in phonics, and we obtained books which, though not perhaps of any great interest in themselves, had at least the advantage of looking academically respectable, a quality which had eluded our program thus far. A fairly engaging series of *"Phonics First"* booklets led tutors and children away from the boring word lists and the contorted sentences with which we began to a sense of accomplishment at actually having finally finished reading a booklet.

Thus, everyone was at least at work, but after less than a year of this, I had begun to doubt our effectiveness and to wonder how we might improve our methods. The children liked their tutors, and eventually worked with them, but the books they were using seemed the least interesting part of the lessons and didn't seem to be doing as much good as I had expected. "It's all so b-o-r-i-n-g," one child regularly objected. To tell the truth, it had begun to seem that way to me as well, and it was not difficult to notice that the method we were seeking to apply depended at least in part on the personality and industry of the tutor who applied it. One ten-year-old boy, who seemed to be what we confidently called an emergent reader, responded well enough to his tutor, but had a kind of engaging if childish irony — "Huh, a doctor who cut open a cat to save a rat that the cat ate by mistake. Who wrote this story?" -- that he often turned against the not very complicated books his tutor, loyally following the program, offered him to read.

In the beginning, however, none of this seemed to matter. We were working at Sursum Corda, a complicated urban community by any standard, with some residents who were said to have been involved in the drug trade, but whose children were engaging, happy, and in need of our support. Still, when we began work, there was about a murder a month in the community -- all drug assassinations, we were assured, so nothing to do with us. Many were revenge killings of those who had themselves committed drug-related murders. Most took place in the small hours, and when the children got up in the morning, they would see the blood being washed down, and hear the latest story, which they would sometimes repeat to their Georgetown tutors.

From the first, I was concerned about the effect this was having on our young learners, and came to detect in some of them a sense of what I came to call "futurelessness," a sense that permeated certain of their attitudes and relationships, and I began to think that, at least in part, our program should consider how we might address it.

One other early problem concerned my own role. In recent years, Georgetown, like other increasingly pre-professional universities, had quietly deemphasized the role of faculty advisor, largely because it envisioned a different role for the faculty than the one that academic professionalism suggested. Increasingly, undergraduate activities outside the classroom had become largely, but not simply, opportunities for students to succeed, or occasionally fail, but to be themselves without interference of any sort, to operate unencumbered by superfluous advice or supervision. Where faculty advisors did remain, the post was, (except in athletics, where it was well paid), simply advisory: if the students sought advice, the advisor supplied it; if not, not.

Often enough, this may have seemed a reasonable policy. The undergraduate literary magazine, which I advised for some years, used to be called the *Georgetown Journal*, published since 1872, and was, after the *Yale Lit* (which has had a somewhat grander if even more complicated recent history), the second oldest undergraduate literary magazine in the country. After a strong effort that was required to reestablish it after a twelve-year lapse, the work of editing became the student editors' alone, and my role became largely to offer advice and occasional support when times were hard. Sometimes, to be sure, things went wrong. An issue was missed, a student's ego was bruised (usually by another student), a manuscript went astray. These things happen, but the world goes on: in the end, an undergraduate literary magazine is there for the students to contend with (and sometimes for). They are the reason for its being, and it is their interests that are served.

But alas! A few years after I handed the operation over to students, it changed its name, shifted to a different schedule, and then ceased publishing altogether. Every so often it springs to life again, usually for an issue or two, but then lapses again into silence. A pity. No more than a campus newspaper, universities like Georgetown should have a continuously published literary magazine in order to encourage student writers.

But my experience with the literary magazine would prove useful to our tutoring program, since in due course we adopted a whole language teaching strategy I had encountered at Berkeley: the practice of issuing a "literary magazine" for Sursum Corda, in order to publish, primarily for parents, caregivers and the learners themselves, a specimen of their work. With the quickening pace of our learners' ability to read and write, our publication schedule (twice yearly) was at least as regular as that of Georgetown's *Anthem* (as the university's sadly kaput literary magazine was last named).

The re-revised Sursum Corda program worked best with about twenty-five pairs of tutors and learners, so that I could keep a sympathetic but unintrusive directive eye on most efforts, while also encouraging the sort of interaction and exchange that became central to what we did. For that reason, we moved away from encouraging our tutors to assemble corrected collections (or portfolios) of their learners' work, as we had in an earlier revision of our program, embracing instead the small, stapled magazines of 16 to 24 pages I have just mentioned, in which the learners' contributions were supplemented by a paragraph from the tutors, commending their learners as specifically as possible, thanking their parents and caregivers, and making plain to one and all what we were about. Commendation of our learners apart, I asked our tutors to also report their own names, majors, years, and hometowns, so as to introduce themselves to the community of Sursum Corda, many of whose members read the magazine through. This is a practice I still find useful today, when fewer and fewer of our students can elect my course more than once or twice.

But in the early days, before we met with our learners twice a week, things were less formal, though perhaps also less effective. From the very late 1980s and well into the 1990s, tutors sought assiduously to become engaged in their learners' early reading progress. In doing so, they depended, in varying degrees, on their understanding of the complex place that Sursum Corda had become, even though otherwise they came to their duties somewhat unformed, and usually required both moral and academic encouragement if they were to be genuinely helpful. In due course we established student officers, and often a student director or two as well, and they too sometimes found informed knowledge and encouragement useful.

There are now courses at Georgetown and elsewhere that are relevant to programs like the one I have been describing. For example, at Boston College, my *alma mater*, a number of philosophy and theology courses are taught that more or less directly support and inform students in such programs. We do not have that depth of instruction at Georgetown, but in due course we were able to join class and program. Initially, our modest attempt at doing so ran into difficulties having to do with our being too directive of the students, and not allowing them to "find their own way." These objections, quite the opposite of what we formerly had heard from the left, were sometimes fed by administrators who did not welcome faculty involvement in curriculum design, which they believed to be their turf, though they did not themselves show much academic interest.

There was, however, a grain of truth in their objections. Education, as Thoreau insisted, is not simply what happens in the classroom, but neither is it innocent of book-learning. Throughout the life of the Sursum Corda program, it was commercial children's books that worked most effectively, though for a time at the beginning we also made collections of our learner's writings, and always employed these imperfectly constructed Informal Reading Inventories (IRI) as part of our practice. As our program developed however, we moved away from IRIs, partly because they proved of limited usefulness with a changing body of tutors, and partly because they seemed a little pretentious given what we were then about.

One of our challenges, though we did not know it at the time, was what seemed to be our initial success. Not only were our undergraduate tutors alert, perceptive, and enthusiastic, they were also numerous. Recruitment was not a problem. At one point, not long after we began, we were able to send as many as thirty students a night to Sursum Corda to work with an equal number of learners. After an initial period of adjustment (it lasted more than a year), and after I returned from first one, then several years of taking summer school courses at Berkeley, we gradually adjusted the focus and direction of our program, embracing a modified version of what we bravely called "whole language teaching," initially including an IRI for each learner, executed by his or her tutor.

The influence of whole language teaching was attractive because it moved us away from the "drill and kill" practices with which we had been flirting. Whole language is an approach to the teaching of reading that emphasizes how the act of reading involves a personally ascertained meaning, and whatever its challenges, it is far from a plodding search for the right word. Its concern is with meaningful acquisition, and it proved particularly valuable with the children with whom we worked, since its precepts were virtually unknown in their schools. For many of these children, television and video-games were the most engaging ways of exploring a world beyond the one that confronted them daily. Against these two delights, however, whole language stands a chance. It engages children by leading them into the whole process of reading, and, in that process, the important satisfaction of comprehension, a satisfaction that rises, in time, to the level of pleasure.

George Bernard Shaw insisted that "Every profession is a conspiracy against the layman," and while I do not wish to deny that whole language can be made to appear wonderfully complex in its shift from charts and tables to interaction and exchange, one of its advantages has always seemed to me its humane understanding of the need for engaging the learner in addressing this thing called life, a need that touches tutor and learner alike, and that concept, in moderation, also informed our program.

And yet we tried not to view whole language as a panacea, as it sometimes was, as a key that would undo all locks. In retrospect, this practice seems to have been wise, since during the time our program began operations, pedagogical thinking was moving away from viewing phonics and whole language as absolutely opposed to each other, but rather as complimentary, each one having something to contribute to the development of reading in many a young child. Our practice was disparage neither, but due to the circumstances in which we worked, we gradually moved toward a modified, by which I mean a simplified, version of whole language, one that focused on interaction and comprehension most of all, and that our tutors could execute with the real but limited instruction I was able to provide.

When we sought to instruct our youngest learners, aged 4 or 5 years old, we would employ such strategies as echo reading, voice pointing, and word sorts, but the tutors who taught young children would seek to establish an understanding of sound-letter relationships early on – starting with consonants, moving on to vowels – along with comprehension, and would do so from the first. But as time went on and our learners became older, phonics decreased in usefulness, even before the move to Golden Rule, and it became increasingly important to be sure the learner understood the meaning of the words he or she was reading, and was interested in them as well. But I must not claim too great an expertise on the part of our tutors in either strategy, except to report that, working with K-6 learners as we were, our focus became largely on comprehension, and that focus, though it did not reject an often limited investment in phonics when called for, had its roots in whole language.

But this pleasure is not a by-product of whole language; rather it is an important part of what it seeks to accomplish, sometimes against the odds. It believes that reading is a natural process, not one crafted and imposed, and that the conditions for learning to speak are similar, in many ways, to those of learning to read. It argues that children come to school already knowing a good deal about reading (though not always "correctly"), and that the act of writing will deepen and develop the ability to read. It places a premium on trust between teacher and student, as good teaching always has, and encourages both the student and the teacher to take risks. And very often, it works!

When I first encountered whole language, it was usual to refer to its projected "empowerment" of the child, and that was a word I used myself, probably too often. In the strictest sense, that is of course what we mean to accomplish: I remember being struck more than once by the way a child became more confident, less worried, happier, when he or she began to read, and that what mattered was not simply that a skill had been acquired, but also that a wider community had been embraced. Still, in the face of video games and television it is a mistake simply to insist on power. Something deeper and more personal must be engaged as well, a kind of strength that issues from the self-actualization that reading brings. It is not the end purpose of reading to encourage a skill so much as to awaken our latent selves, and to suggest connections. Language is social, and any act of reading is an act of both participation and interpretation.

When we began organizing the program in a way that took into account some elements from whole language, it was clear that we would need new books, and would need to address our tutors' work differently. We wanted to begin with the children as early as possible. In practice, that meant beginning at about five years old, though in due course we reached down to four-and-a-half-year-olds. We understood that by that time some attitudes towards literacy were already developing (at as early as three years old, many children can identify logos, places, teams, and brand names), but hoped that by reaching out to very young children we could engage them in one way or another. One way of doing so was to read to them, and to try to identify any interests an individual child might have. An eight-year-old I taught at Berkeley, for example, was much taken with dinosaurs and mermaids, and though neither figured among the topics that interested the children we worked with at Sursum Corda (who had other monsters to contend with), it was not difficult to identify topics that did -- the Washington Redskins and (to the surprise of some of the tutors) the Dallas Cowboys, for example, or the Georgetown basketball team (the Hoyas), or sometimes animals, though usually not dogs or cats.

This seemed particularly important because it became apparent early on that the encounters many children had with literacy in their formative years had not been particularly interesting to them. At a Christmas party at the end of our first semester, one of our tutors was proudly explaining to a parent about the way the boy he was tutoring was now reading, only to be told that what was important was arithmetic, not reading, so that the child would not be cheated when he spent money. (Later, one of our advisors in the community wisely suggested that, in such circumstances, the tutor could reply that the child will have to sign contracts, and so would need to read too.)

In another case a child asked a parent to read one of our books, only to be told that the parent (who had been cheated out of literacy himself) had important things to do and had no time for such foolishness. Newspapers do not appear in Sursum Corda households, nor greeting cards, nor very many books. The Bible is present, owned and read by grandmothers in particular and usefully observed doing so by her grand-children. But opportunities for the children to learn the use-fulness, let alone the pleasure, of reading were not so very many. Our tutors needed to start at the beginning.

Fortunately, their great allies in the undertaking proved to be the children. Bright, eager, and captivating, they brought a joy and an energy to the tutorials that few of the tutors -- themselves disposed to hope for and to believe the best — could possibly resist. We learned to draw upon that energy and sought to make the process of reading a part of -- not apart from -- their very active lives. When it worked, it was great. We tried to get each child to write or at least to draw a picture from a story he or she had read or listened to, and to process what had been learned: for example, to draw a pic-ture of what happened the next day when the boy or girl in the story saw the lion again.

In doing so, we began with what the great New Zealand teacher and theorist Marie Clay designated as the "Concepts About Print," but to do it in a way that encouraged play as much as industry. We were concerned, of course, that the very youngest children learn to turn pages, to distinguish letters and know whether they were capital or small, to understand what words are and how they remain constant as they move across the page, and what it means for a story (and a sen-tence) to come to an end. But in our better moments, we tried to make knowledge come as easily as may be, and by practice, not precept. Even when teaching letters of the alphabet, we encouraged tutors to be imaginative, to use letters on cards to spell the child's name and other names as well: McDonalds, for example, or Sursum Corda.

But in practice, when it comes to *p* and *b* or *d, m* or *n*, science flourishes, and precept carries the day. Students who took the course I offered (in the beginning about a quarter of the tutors, now one and all) carried on with what is called phonemic segmentation, which helps to distinguish phonemes. The practice seemed to work best with slightly older children, who can distinguish between phonemes and letters. The tutors also worked with invented spelling, essentially asking children to spell words they did not know as they sounded, to assess whether the students could recognize phonemes. Some tutors preferred the more game-like repetition of sounds in a given list of words. But even these tutors understood how the process worked and developed it at will. Now at Golden Rule, working with older and more advanced learners, such practices have been less often required.

A more complicated matter was the way in which we used stories, particularly with beginning readers, of which we had many early on at Sursum Corda. We had, in those early days, and thanks to two generous grants from the Hillsdale Foundation, been able to expand our library, and many of the tutors made effective use of it, finding stories of interest to their learners, using previewing and predicting strategies to engage them as deeply as possible in what was going on, and, most importantly, to incite interest whenever possible.

Previewing (going over a narrative with a very young reader before reading it, identifying names and difficult words) and predicting (pausing, usually at a suspenseful point, to ask what is going to happen next) were central to the teaching we did, which sought to engage higher-thinking faculties as soon as and as often as possible. From the very beginning, even before my course came into being, we encouraged all our tutors to look over the book with their learners, and to discuss what it seemed to be about; to look at the pictures, and to say what they suggested; to identify the protagonist and to envision him or her, and so on. Once the learner was reading (assisted by the tutor in this example), it became the tutor's role to help the student advance to higher thinking, the metacognitive level, and to ask questions: What does the learner think will happen next; what would happen if two of the characters were to meet; what would the learner say if, on the way home, he or she met that rabbit? If the learner was reluctant to answer, or gave only silly answers, as sometimes happened, we encouraged the tutor to take out a notebook and to write down exactly what the child had to say, so that if the response was right (or near enough), the answer could be looked up in the story just read, and the answer applauded. Sometimes, particularly with young learners, at the end of the reading the tutor asked the learner to draw a picture of some event in the story, and write what it was under it, even if the learner did not yet know how to read or write. The writing which thus emerged sometimes offered valuable clues to the extent of the young learner's understanding of Marie Clay's Concepts About Print, or simply about how far he or she understood the story.

Other times we asked the child to tell a story, and his or her tutor would write it down. At the next tutorial, the tutor would bring the story back, now typed up (or these days, word processed), and tutor and learner would read and discuss it together. The results of these "dictated stories" was mixed, and more than one child was unwilling to speak at any length at all, so that the whole exercise would be wound up in a single sentence. Thus, carefully, they taught their tutors patience. To counter this particular difficulty, a few tutors, and I myself, would sometimes write stories in which the learner himself or herself appeared as a principal character, together with a friend. This could be helpful with beginning readers, once the first breakthrough had been made.

Some, though by no means all, of the stories would take the learner away from Sursum Corda and on a trip, though they would bring him or her back at the end. This was a practice I myself employed with a young learner I was then teaching. But the stories themselves were often informed by known texts. To compare small things with great, "Jimmy and the Loch Ness Monster," my composition, was influenced by Steven Crane's "The Blue Hotel," one of my own favorite short stories, though I admit the connection is not readily apparent. But in Crane's fiction, the reader is greeted by one surprise, one frustrated expectation after another, and that was what I was aiming at there. Boys from Sursum Corda do not regularly travel to Scotland or address a monster in the argot of a British schoolboy of the last century, but that didn't seem to matter; indeed it only added to a sense of intelligible difference. The story was influenced too by one of the tutors, a young woman who had come to study at Georgetown for a year from Glasgow University. She had been tutoring a somewhat difficult learner, whom she had taught with sensitivity, tact, and care. In a way, the story was a tribute to her work and her success.

In another story, "The Necessary Elephant," I used not only St. Thomas More's scholastic dictum concerning the usefulness to humankind of all created things, but also, and even more incongruously, lines that had always amused me from John Milton's *Paradise Lost*: "Gambold before them [Adam and Eve], th' unwieldy Elephant / To make them mirth us'd all his might, & wreathd / His lithe Proboscis" (Book IV, lines 345-47). I read the lines, I doubt originally, as indicating that, to Milton at least, the purpose of the elephant's trunk (his "proboscis") was to amuse the human beings with whom he shared a yet-uncorrupted world. But I am no Miltonist, so no doubt more profound readings are possible. Nonetheless, I have printed the stories below, and as I am transcribing them, recall that the learner for whom I wrote them much preferred the trip to Scotland, and only shook his head at the elephant, having never seen one in Sursum Corda.

Jimmy and the Loch Ness Monster

One time, Jimmy and his friend Claud decided to take a trip, so they went to Scotland. Scotland is a very beautiful country almost three hundred miles long, which is to the north of England. It has many mountains, islands and lakes (lakes are called "lochs" in Scotland), many sheep and cows, and much beautiful countryside. Its capital is called Edinburgh, and it is one of the most beautiful cities in the world. Sometimes it rains in Scotland, but not very much.

Jimmy and Claud heard that there was a monster in one of the lakes, the one called Loch Ness, so they thought they would go out and see if they could make friends with it. They waited a great long time by the wonderful lake, but they didn't see anything but water and sky.

"I'm tired of waiting," Claud said, "this is boring. Perhaps this monster doesn't exist at all. Let's go back to Edinburgh and have some fun."

"No, please," said Jimmy, "just a little while longer. I'm sure he'll come if we wait."

Just then Jimmy and Claud both saw a bulge on the shore. It was green and quivering and horrible, and they both thought it was the monster. They ran over to it at once.

"Hello, Sir," said Claud. "How are you?"

"Oh no," said the horrible green bulge. "I might have known it would be you two. Well, I'm fine. How are you?"

Then they looked again and saw it was only George, who had disguised himself to look like a little monster.

"Why, George," said Claud, "what a surprise to see you here! Have you been here a long time? And why are you dressed like that?"

"Honestly," said George. "I give up on both of you. Isn't it obvious what I'm doing? Well, perhaps not. Very well then, I'll try to explain it to you, but do pay attention. Now then. Ahem. Shortly after I arrived here, I spent many uneventful days waiting for this stupid monster to appear. He didn't. I was becoming skeptical about him. He may not exist at all, you know. Then I thought, Ah ha! I'll dress up like a little monster, and then he'll come to visit me. It was a great idea, if I do say so myself, but all I caught was you two. I wanted to catch him to have him for dinner. Now I'll have to go back to using a fishing pole. Do you know if monsters like worms?"

"I don't think you should be trying to kill the poor old thing," said Jimmy. "And besides, I think it's very rude to catch people with a hook, especially when you've never even met them."

"I agree," said Claud, "and don't forget that you're a guest in his country. He's probably Scottish, you know, and it would be the meanest thing in the world if you ate him for dinner. How would you feel if he wanted to eat you?"

"Oh nonsense," said George. "I'll do what I like. If he's Scottish I bet he'll taste good."

"Oh, but I'm not Scottish at all," said a voice over their shoulder. "I'm English, though I've been living in Scotland for the longest time and rather liking it. The water is so much better up here, you know. So's the air."

They looked around and saw it was the Loch Ness monster. He was very big and green, but he looked rather old and tired as well.

"Hello," said Jimmy. "It's very nice to make your acquaintance. My name's Jimmy, and that's my friend Claud. Oh yes. And that's George."

"Pleased to meet you, I'm sure," said the monster. "Welcome to Scotland. If you don't mind, I think I'll eat George for supper."

"Oh, eat him?" said Jimmy. "Well, I really don't know. To

tell the truth I really don't think you should. He'd probably only give you a stomachache, you know."

"I would not!" cried George. "What a horrible thing to say. What makes you think I'd give him a stomachache, anyway? You two will say anything."

"Now I'm really confused," said the monster. "I don't know who's right and who's wrong. Well, I may just give him a nibble then, to see what he tastes like. I only come out of the loch once every hundred years, you know. Just long enough to grab a snack. Then back I go again. Stand clear now."

"Ach now, Nessie, stand fast," said another voice. "Ye know better than that. Off with ye now. Scat. Back into the loch."

"Who are you?" said the three boys together.

"Oh, that's Robert Bruce," said the monster. "He and I are old friends. He's been around for centuries, too. Chases off people who try to catch me. Chases me off when I try to eat people. You know how it is. Well, rules are rules. Must be off. Very nice to meet you. Bye."

And with that the monster jumped back into the loch and swam away.

"Ach, boys," said Robert Bruce, "no more silly tricks now. George, you especially. But I heard you talking. Off to Edinburgh, is it? No such thing. There's a town even more beautiful than Edinburgh, and Glasgow it's called. You'll have even more fun there. Off with you now."

So Jimmy and Claud went off to Glasgow and they took George too, because they were afraid if they didn't he would make a lot of trouble for Robert Bruce, who seemed like a very nice man. They all had a great time in Glasgow, and then they came home to Sursum Corda.

The End

Jimmy and the Necessary Elephant

One day Jimmy noticed that there was a large grey elephant standing in front of the Community Center at Sursum Corda. It had enormous ears, and a tiny tail, but it had too a most wonderful trunk, and that was what interested Jimmy. He called his friend Claud over and asked him where it came from. Claud said he didn't know, but that it had been there for a day or so, and everybody seemed to like it. Nobody was paying it much attention now, so Jimmy and Claud went over to it.

"Hello, Elephant," said Jimmy, "I'm Jimmy and that's my friend Claud. What's your name?"

But the elephant didn't say anything, and the boys guessed that it was probably a real elephant, not a magic one, and that it couldn't talk.

"Well, it's much better to have a real elephant," said Claud. "At least that way he won't be able to disappear when we're not looking."

"Yes," said Jimmy, "but who's going to feed it, and give it water? And anyway, why does it have that wonderful trunk? It makes me happy just to look at it, but what good is it?"

"Search me," said Claud. "We can ask some people if you want, maybe somebody knows."

"Well, don't ask me," said a voice behind them. "That's the silliest question I ever heard. Why does an elephant have a trunk, indeed? It just does, that's all. What's the matter with you two, anyway? Elephants always have trunks. It's what makes them elephants. I think I'll tell you all about elephants. Now then. Ahem."

"Hello, George," said both boys together.

"What are you doing here?" said Claud. "I thought you didn't like big animals."

"Don't normally," said George. "Made an exception for this one. It's not a dog you know, and I mean to bring it some water. I might be friends with it or I might eat it. I really can't make up my mind. Do either of you know how elephants taste? No, probably you don't."

"Oh honestly, George," said Jimmy. "Always thinking of food. What's the matter with you? Bring it some water if you like. The poor old thing looks thirsty. But I don't think you'll like it any better than you did the Loch Ness monster."

"Really, Jimmy," said George. "Must you bring that up? We all make mistakes. You two make millions of them, I bet. Well, OK, I think I'll give the poor old thing some water."

"That's good," said Claud, as George squirted some water from a hose into the large tub by the elephant's feet. "But who shall we ask about the trunk?"

Just then Sister Roche came along, and Jimmy and Claud ran over to ask her why the elephant has a trunk.

"Well, I'm not sure I know the whole answer," Sister Roche said. "But a great man named Sir Thomas More who lived five hundred years ago..."

"He's probably been dead for some time," put in George, who had finished filling the tub and come over to the group.

"Yes, I believe he is," Sister Roche agreed. "Well, he said that God made flowers for their beauty, animals for their innocence, and men and women to serve Him wittily, in the tangle of their minds. He meant that everything has a purpose, you see. Flowers are beautiful, animals are fun, and people intelligent."

"Huh, well these two have the most tangled minds I've ever seen," said George. "But I'm not sure that means they're intelligent."

"Oh, George," said Sister Roche. "But there's something else, you know. Just looking at the trunk makes me feel happy. It's so funny! That seems to me a very good reason to have a trunk, if it makes people feel happy."

"I agree," said Jimmy. "That's an excellent reason. It makes me happy just to see him wave it."

"Oh nonsense," said George. "I don't feel happy at all. That's just, you know, an idea."

But just then the elephant scooped up some water, and squirted George with his trunk. Everybody laughed, even (after a second or two) George himself, and then Jimmy understood why it was necessary for elephants to have trunks, and for people to be happy as they can.

The End

I wrote these stories, which first appeared in an earlier account of Sursum Corda (*Sursum Corda. Teaching Urban Youth to Read,* Georgetown University Press, 1992, pp. 73-74, 77-78), when we were still working out how we might proceed, but even after changes had been made to our program, these stories still did echo the strategies with which we were always concerned. Apart from introducing certain words to the child I was instructing, there was no palpable purpose in them except to engage and amuse my learner. It was clear to me from the first that they were more attractive than word lists, and my excellent learner took to them with a will.

This pleasure of reading in the company both of a tutor and of others no doubt contributed to our success. But one problem we discovered was that familiarity could breed contempt as well as friendship, particularly as our program grew in size, from ten, to twenty, to thirty, and more. Once they had established a bond with their learners, the tutors sometimes relaxed, and were not as rigorous or as attentive as when they had begun. As a guard against this contingency we instituted, for a certain period, what we called a weekly log, designed to encourage the tutor to think through and prepare the lesson in advance, and to consider what worked and what didn't.

Sursum Corda-Georgetown University
Youth Tutoring Program
Weekly Log

Name of Tutor:_____Learner:_____Date:___

	Time: Projected/Actual	Results
High-interest Material Tutor Reads to Learner		
Learner Rereads Familiar Material		
Word Games/ Voice Pointing Word Sorting Echo Reading		
Writing/ Drawing (Based on Reading)		
Reading New Material		
Other Your choice! Be inventive!		

This regard for individual accomplishment produced some interesting problems. Toward the beginning of the reorganization, one of the officers in the Office of Student Affairs got in touch to ask how we planned to test the children and asked for copies of the results. The reasons he gave seemed to him logical enough: he was applying for grants, and he wanted to say, "Look, this is how the children were before they were tutored, here they are now, see what good results these are, and please give us as much money as possible," or words to that effect.

Still, I was not much taken with what he wanted to do. For one thing, it seemed to me unacceptable to hand over test results of Sursum Corda children to an official who wanted to use them to enrich the university, even in the interest of our learners. I understood, of course, that the argument continues that the university is in turn enriching the community, but what was sought was more personal than any information to which a right could be claimed, and I thought the request unconsidered. I also thought the information we would be likely to acquire would be wildly inaccurate, unless of course we followed the uncomplicated pattern of progress and reward which the official had described.

But quite apart from any ethical or social consideration, it is simply not possible (or particularly desirable) to organize a relatively large group of student tutors so that each one administers and assesses a test accurately, with the results being compatible.

The advance that many of our learners made was gradual and slow, exactly the sort of progress that Marie M. Clay pointed out in *Becoming Literate* (1991, p. 204). Standardized tests have many difficulties in measuring change, a concern now widely understood. A sensitive and perceptive teacher, on the other hand, can see progress before it shows up in any test, and that is what, whether naively or not, we wanted to make our tutors become.

That is not say, of course, that anything went. But we sought to focus our strategies on the tutors as well as on the learners, so as not to pretend to more than we could accomplish, out of respect for the learners whom we served. I understand that this could not apply to teachers in schools, and that, over-tested though American children may be, some form of measurement can hardly be avoided. But student tutors should not pretend to a competence they do not have. Once measurements are instituted, they, and not the learners, can easily become the reason for the program's being. Furthermore, in programs that involve student teachers, it is the student teachers, rather than the learners, at whom the tests are effectively directed, much in the same way that in some places full-time teachers are the ones who are held accountable for their students' performance on standardized tests, whatever other circumstances may be involved. That is why in literacy support groups like those I have been discussing, where student-learner exchange is itself an important element of the program, it is the teachers, whom we call the tutors, toward whom measurements should be directed. My experience has been that once the program's objectives are understood, students welcome whatever instruction is forthcoming. Just as a football team functions better with than without a coach, so a student tutorial program functions best when the tutors, as well as the learners, are encouraged, supported and, in their case at least, measured. It can be a mistake for courses like the ones I have been describing here to test or measure the learners, and so lay claim to a higher degree of professionalism than they in fact enjoy.

Apart from anything else, it establishes a different relationship between the engaged learner and the sensitively overseen tutor. Such measurement should be the property of schools, not the programs, which exist rather to engage, to instruct, sometimes to delight, and always to entertain those whom they seek to serve. But where money is involved, I understand of course that this perspective may not pass unchallenged.

We took student writing more and more seriously as we progressed, experimenting with collections of learner writing which, as I have indicated, eventually led us to produce what we grandly called a literary magazine, so as to give the texts we produced wider circulation. The two items that follow may help indicate the sort of work that emerged.

My Favorite Poet

My favorite poet is Langston Hughes. Langston Hughes is the best poet I ever read about. I love Langston Hughes a lot and I wish he never died in 1967. My best poem is Midnight Raffle. The most part I liked was the second stanza, which reads:

I lost my nickel,
I lost my time,
I got back home,
Without a dime.

Why is he my favorite Poet? Because he writes more short poems than long ones. He was a good playwright too. He is the best poet in my life. Also, I like Robert Frost.

Perhaps not flawless, but I promised warts as well, and it seems at least as felt as many a term paper I have read. But a longer and more considered piece of prose was this one:

Basketball Games (Trojans)

Trojans (#2) are a ten and under team of the Metropolitan Police Boys & Girls Club. The Trojans didn't have a good year but we won against #6 and had a close game against #12. I write about them because they were good games and nobody played dirty, and we won one game and lost seven.

The team was a good team but we didn't get a chance to practice. We have a couple of good men named: Derek, Kelvin and Earl. Earl Risby is good on defense and sometimes on offence. He has good control of the ball but he needs an open shot to shoot. Derek Pigford, and Kelvin Black are good at offense and sometimes defense. Kelvin got mad but he is happy now, Derek is the man who is wide open on the basketball court. Derek and Kelvin are in the same class, also same school that I go to: Walker-Jones Elementary School.

How did I get in the game? I got in the game because my coach Jimmy let me in the game. Jimmy is a good coach. Sometimes he is hard on us, but I like him anyway.

This is the game with #12. I scored 4 points, 4 rebounds, no blocks and one foul. My total career high was 4 points, 4 rebounds, no blocks, and three fouls.

Since the last game we lost against #8. The score was 18 to 20.

In all games we end it like this: we shake hands and go home for tutoring. I hope we do better next year.

This could of course be edited and discussed, and for a period such texts served their purpose, even as they gave way to focusing on a single important piece of writing to which tutor and learner could return together, one that would appear in print in our little magazine. The main difficulty we had with writing and rewriting texts was that too great an emphasis upon them could swamp the tutorial and make everything else seem less important. Perhaps because most undergraduates attach a high degree of attention to the papers they write, too much writing, useful though it was, could attract so much industry, often on the tutor's part, that reading practice seemed to diminish. The real audience for our learners' work was their community, their parents or caregivers, they themselves, and their tutors, too. The point of a literary magazine like the one we published is not that it become part of a student record, but that it be a pleasure to write for and to edit or construct, and that it be waved about and shown to parents and caregivers, uncles and aunts, friends and other tutors – indeed to any who are interested.

One other concern that engaged us in those early days was prior knowledge, which has an important place in our story. As a community, Sursum Corda was neither apathetic nor ravaged, as outside groups that sought to impose a new order upon it quickly learned. Rather it was a powerful and even impressive community, right up to the end, one in which many groups and persons cooperated and contended. Some of these relationships involved the drug trade, where disputes could be final, others internecine, and rarely violent. Although our tutors were largely insulated from the former, the children they taught were not, and any attempt by the tutors to understand their learners' world had to take many things into account. These included their learners' families, both near and extended, the houses in which they lived -- the best thing Sursum Corda had to offer, according to many learners -- their school, their friends, their teams, even their tutors. But the effects of the drug trade were present before them, and, as we shall see in subsequent chapters, resonated in their lives. That is why they are mentioned here. If prior knowledge meant anything, it meant, for all of us, that too.

Chapter 2

The Way We Were

1. What Literacy Is, and Why

I came late to the study of literacy, but from the earliest days I wondered not only how it came about, but also how illiteracy played out in our social roles, day-to-day. This interest, which became a concern, came home to me during 1989, our first year working at Sursum Corda, when we discovered one ten-year-old boy who had been in the program for over a year, and yet knew next to nothing about how to read, a circumstance of which his previous tutor had been unaware. Not only did the boy not know the alphabet, but even Marie Clay's "Concepts About Print," the rules teaching how print works, were simply unknown to him. He was an expert dawdler; he would entreat to have a book read to him and would respond to it with apparent interest. There were even one or two pamphlets that he had effectively memorized. His former tutor had been teaching him how to function as an illiterate in a literate world, one of our advisors reasonably argued.

He of course attracted our attention, but I wondered how many others like him there were in the city. Illiteracy is a topic on which historians disagree, though in fact, when looking at other places and times, circumstances differ so markedly that it is difficult to make any meaningful generalizations. Often, we are reduced to individual cases in particular places, even when we know that there was a lot of illiteracy around. Was Alfred the Great's "notebook," as it has been called, really a collection of texts he inscribed because they pleased him, or an aid to his developing literacy? When, in nineteenth-century America, Frederic Douglass was denied further instruction, had not his first instructor, Mrs. Auld, already instructed him so effectively in the then unknown Concepts About Print that he could thereafter seize control of his own learning? The ability to read is such an individual activity that we still underestimate its social effect. This proposition was made clear to me in the summer of 1990, when I spent about four weeks in the country that was then still called Czechoslovakia. There, I came to understand better than I had before what it means to be illiterate, and what compensates for it.

I neither speak nor read Czech or Russian (almost a second language there), and so was restricted in my contacts to those who spoke English or French. My destination was Palacky University in Olomouc, and until I was established there, I did not really understand what it meant to live in a place where most books were closed to me, and where my friendships and my contacts were circumscribed by language. Later, alone in Prague, I came to understand, but I noticed as well that circumstances had brought me one great compensation: the strength of the dollar. Not long before I'd arrived, the exchange rate had risen from sixteen crowns to the dollar to just over twenty-five, a shift dramatic enough to make me feel reasonably well off despite the fact that I really didn't have a large amount of money. But I could not help feeling too, in a way I do not like to contemplate, that my apparent affluence gave strength to my otherwise confused spirit, and I understood that if one cannot read, money becomes a compelling necessity, whatever its source.

I was back in Washington in the fall, and not long after had a talk with one of the two student leaders of our program about what we needed to do in the upcoming year. We agreed that we should concern ourselves even more with the continuous training of the tutors, but then he added that we needed to do more with the children outside of the tutorials, and should have more outings, more activities. The difficulty was, as it still is, in getting our tutors to commit themselves to Saturday excursions, since most of them live busy lives indeed. But he pointed out that we did not need all the tutors on each trip, as had been our labor-intensive practice in the past. What we needed was some kind of formal structure to encourage informality with regularity. Although we did not come to any great conclusion, we agreed in the end that our talk had been usefully negative.

In the rest of this chapter, and also in the next one, I have written about our program and the community of Sursum Corda in a series of what I call gobbits: short, self-contained but loosely connected narratives, some close together in time, some months or years apart, that I recorded off and on in a diary that focused exclusively on our program. These seek to reveal how it was that we encountered and understood the community of Sursum Corda, no doubt imperfectly in many cases, and what outcomes we experienced and produced. The word gobbit, as used in Oxford, designates a short passage of verse or prose, usually placed on a college or university examination for students to translate or comment upon or both. The gobbits that follow, however, are drawn from life, not literature, and are, in their way, often both the question posed and the answer offered. Given the circumstances in which we worked, and what we did and sought to do, these gobbits, which are narratively separate but culturally connected, seem to me the best way to illustrate the workings of the program in its last twenty-seven years.

2. How We Met Each Other

Two of the student leaders and I returned the books we had kept in my office over the summer, and afterwards had lunch with Allene at Decateurs. We are all in good form, and Allene, the sharp, kind, African-American woman whom the university had engaged to work with the parents and care-givers of our learners, told us this story: Earlier in the summer she had asked a little boy what he was going to be when he grew up. "I don't know," he replied, "I live at Sursum Corda." Allene was the wrong person to whom to say that, and she at once took him up on what he had implied, insisting that his answer had nothing to do with her question, and he could be anything he wanted to be. But of course, as she knew well, he was indeed answering her question. Not everyone here has a future, he pointed out to her.

Partly as a result of our conversation, I went down to Sursum Corda the next day to see Allene again, and to get from her the list of the new year's learners. At one point she was holding the list of pupils, I the list of tutors, and I asked which learner we should give to Al, one of our livelier tutors. "Let's give Al to..." she replied, and I was reminded how race touches everything we do. I was inclined to give the child to the tutor, while Allene gave the tutor to the child!

Not all of our assignments went smoothly. The next Thursday I went down to meet Alan, one of the boys I planned to tutor myself, having chosen him because I had learned that there were difficulties with his progress. His previous tutor was spending the semester in Czechoslovakia, but Alan certainly needed to continue in the program. It turned out that, although ten years old, he could barely read on the primer level, and even his pre-primer was none too secure. This is a shock and surprise; it was as though he had made no progress at all. Still, he had not read all summer, and I thought that that circumstance might account for it. But I was concerned with some of the mistakes he made, which were very elementary, and wondered if there were other factors at work as well.

3. Our Learners' World

In the early days in our program I tutored along with the students, partly to learn what was actually involved in the process. Very soon, I began to like the young man with whom I was working, who was 8 years old. Some weeks after we had begun working together, our talk took a sudden turn. In the middle of our lesson, he suddenly told me about a dream he'd had a night ago in which he had been in school, and his teacher had come to tell him he was doing badly. He was not surprised, as if some long-known truth suddenly had appeared before him. I heard him out and asked a few questions. He told me there had been a confrontation between another boy and the teacher earlier in the day. Then I told him with all the confidence I could muster how well he was doing now, and how smart he was. I assured him that I wasn't saying that just because I had to say it. He heard me out, then nodded impatiently, and we returned to our lesson.

Meanwhile, at Sursum Corda itself, things had become somewhat more complicated. There had been another murder the Wednesday before, while tutoring was actually going on, and having learned from the police what happened, we left, at their request, half an hour early. Two nights before that, a man was buying drugs at Sursum Corda, but foolishly sought to short-change the sellers by handing them a ten-dollar bill wrapped around several ones, evidently hoping to get away before they discovered the deception. It didn't work. His pursuers ran him down to First and K St. NW and shot him dead.

And this: Two of our tutors had gone to take their learners, who were brothers, to a Saturday movie, having obtained their mother's permission two nights earlier after tutoring. She wasn't there when he and his friend collected their learners on Saturday, but they set out together, and on the way, saw the boys' mother approaching them on a wide sidewalk leading down to Union Station, which in those days still had a cinema. "Look, it's your mother," he said to his learner, who hardly raised his eyes before answering, "No it's not." As they approached the tutor called out a greeting, but the woman, now with glazed eyes, continued on past them.

The young mother of a six-year-old boy in our program had been abandoned by her lover, and so turned to the drug trade to support her habit and her son. But those with whom she now worked used her roughly, hit her, and did so in front of her son, who, attracted to their power and excited by their violence, sought to embrace their behavior in a way that shocked us all.

4. The Things We Did

One of our early trips involved taking fourteen of our younger learners out to the Pet Farm near Reston, Virginia, for what proved a quite hilarious trip. It was in October, and there was a haunted house, Halloween being not far off. But what worried some of the children more than the haunted house were the emus that roamed freely about, as well as a perfectly friendly dog, a gigantic pig, and some horses. The boy I was teaching at the time bounced around quite happily, but for some of the others, the farm was a new world indeed, and one that took some getting used to. But in due course they all did so, and when it was time to go, the ones who had been most taken aback by what they had first seen were the least willing to leave.

And this: when the children were waiting for a pony ride, a middle-aged White woman standing behind them in the line began to complain that our group was taking over, was everywhere at once. "I know what her problem is," said one of our seven-year-olds. "She just doesn't like Black people to be ahead of her in line."

5. Art History

I had picked up one of our more advanced books to work with, and almost passed by a short reading passage on Michelangelo, but the learner I was working with that day spotted it, and immediately wanted to read it, having heard who Michelangelo was. He put on a most scholarly voice, read the passage, and answered the questions at the end with evident interest, pausing only to interrupt himself in order to offer a series of descriptions of God and to talk about Matthew and Luke, all of whom had made their way into the text.

Another time I discussed Christianity with the same learner. Having established that Christ and Jesus were the same person, I had to work against the idea that the boy had somehow gotten into his head that Christ was born in 1759. We had gone to the National Gallery of Art for lunch with another boy and his tutor the week before, and I had been resolved to get us all upstairs to see some paintings, even briefly, before we left. Knowing that the plan was to return to a football game at Sursum Corda immediately after lunch, I pointed out that the most beautiful painting in the world was upstairs, and we could see it before we returned to Sursum Corda, if they had time. "The most beautiful painting in the world?" my learner repeated with doubtful but intrigued emphasis. "Yes, certainly," I maintained, but said again that we really didn't have to go, if they didn't want to. No, no, they both replied.

And so it was that soon after we stood before the large, round, lavishly painted *The Adoration of the Magi*, by Fra Angelico and Fra Lippo Lippi. We counted the figures, puzzled over certain ones, identified the Magi and the event, and agreed that it well deserved its designation.

6. How We Celebrated Halloween

Our Halloween parties in those days were invariably successful, with trick-or-treating for the learners being held on t first floor of Copley (the dormitory floor then reserved for students involved in social action projects), and a party held in Copley Lounge afterwards. All noisy and free. My learner proved adept at blowing bubbles through a circle and won a balloon-whistle; a friend of his tried everything twice, and usually won something. At the end, remembering previous years, I volunteered to go back to Sursum Corda on the bus that brought the children, in order to try to preserve some kind of order. "Good luck," the driver said. He was right; with two student tutors at the front and me at the back, we may have made some difference, but not one you could measure. I came back in a van with a tutor and one of the students who had been with me on the bus, a young Black woman newly arrived at Georgetown, who was very critical of what she had seen. There was too much noise she rightly said, and we needed to do more to make the children socialize better. Life was one great party. She had seen two children fighting at the party and she'd thought that the tutors didn't move quickly enough to break it up.

Reading isn't enough in a program like this one," she'd said. It was all getting too big, she was afraid, and we weren't having the effect we could and should have.

The tutor (and to a lesser extent I: she had been only been singing my song, though a bit too stridently) was taken aback by her outburst, though he recovered quickly enough. He said that some of the children certainly seemed to have been on a candy high, but thought that perhaps we shouldn't attach too much importance to the noise they had made.

r

I had been trying to find new books for the program, particularly for the older children, some of whom had begun to read, and needed slightly more advanced and much more interesting books with which to continue. In doing so, we had been looking less at assorted workbooks than at reading books that focused on the African-American experience.

I had been reading Tana Reiff's *Nobody Knows* (1989), to see if we could use it in our program. It is a narrative that begins in 1902, and traces a girl of six, Mattie, who is discriminated against in a candy store as a child, marries at eighteen and goes to Chicago, where her husband, a union man who "made a better living than most Black men," is attacked and murdered, forcing Mattie to work first in a steel mill, and then (in 1929) as a maid. During World War II things get better, but when her mother (who has been with her in Chicago) dies, she returns home to the South, where she leads a successful demonstration against the candy store which had first discriminated against her. The blurb on the back cover remarks, "Between 1910 and 1950, about 3 1/2 million Black Americans migrated from the South to the North."

It is graphic and true to American history, but how does it touch a child? Clearly its perceptive author intends that the reader should learn about the wrongs done to Blacks in the past, and about their courage and determination in the face of violence in the North as well as in the South. Mattie's life is meant to be hard but typical, with the defeat of the candy store apparently her most important victory.

But I was concerned that it was the continuing failure, rather than the final victory, that ultimately impressed. Despite a few tender moments, Mattie is a victim and is presented to the young reader as such, with an implied invitation to follow her example in confronting her initial oppressor, whom she met in a candy store.

However, it is certainly possible to draw other conclusions from the text. A victim is not required ever to trust an oppressor or to hope for justice from forces as violent as the ones Mattie confronts. There is but one out for her, and any expectation of a better life is deferred to the last page, where it hardly convinces. The account is indeed historical, but would a Black child draw any strength or support from its narrative? What if the child came from an affluent Black family? From a less affluent family? Would the effect be to join the struggle? But is there not some danger that the effect would be exactly the opposite of the one intended? And did it not matter that the person with whom he was reading the book was White?

At the next tutorial I tried to get my learner to read *Nobody Knows*, but after seeing what it was about, he put the book aside and wouldn't read it. I didn't press it for reasons I have described, and also because I had the sense that he had seen something I hadn't. Later, I recalled an incident in volume three of Robert Coles' *Children of Crisis* series, the one called *The South Goes North* (1971). A Black grandmother is driving in the American South with her daughter and granddaughter, and the grandmother starts talking about slave days. But the granddaughter won't listen, sings to herself, and looks out the window, until the grandmother takes her point, and desists, recalling that the old days weren't so great after all. There seemed to me to have been something of that in my learner's reaction, putting his guard up, taking no chances, at least not with me.

8. Why we went to Sursum Corda

It happened especially in our early days that we sometimes would make a breakthrough, in which a learner very suddenly discovered that he or she could read and was as surprised and delighted as his or her astonished tutor. The learner would continue reading for a couple of minutes, find out that it was real, that he or she really could read, and then would run over to his or her friends, who usually would be sitting at another table, to say what had happened and what was now possible.

One time I heard them reply "So can we," but he knew they couldn't and told them so – "No, No, you can't" -- laughing and happy, almost giddy, all the while. His tutor was not less delighted, and hardly knew what to say, but told him they will always be friends, and also what might not have been so: that he would go to Georgetown, and when he was older they would go on dates together, since if he could read, he could do anything.

9. Difference

One night, as I left the Community Center where we worked, there were children standing about outside looking apprehensively at some smoke just visible over in the direction of M Street and First, and one said that the Fire Department was coming. My learner and I made our way up McKenna Walk and across the parking lot, since in those days I was still taking him home after our tutorial, and as we walked, he suddenly said that he wasn't frightened when we were together. When we got to First Street, we looked back, and I saw what was amiss: a couch had been left on the sidewalk and someone had put a match into it. It either was made of a flammable material, or it had been doused, and now bright orange flames were shooting out all around it, brilliantly vivid and in a strange way rather beautiful in the dark night. But my learner had a different reaction and pulled me away.

Two days before, I had been having a hard time getting another learner to work. I would work with several learners in those days. I had read to him from one of our books, the story of Noah, with the reader reminded of all those people God had allowed to die in the flood. But my new learner was much taken by it, and when I offered to read him another story, not wanting to leave him with that alone, he made me read it again.

10. Slow Progress

Difficulties with my new learner had not grown fewer. He had begun reading better than in the beginning of the semester, but he was not there yet, and he knew it, partly because he had a younger brother who now read better and faster than he did. Part of the problem was to convince him that he actually could improve, that he was not stuck where he was, in spite of evidence to the contrary. We had one lesson when he was so fixed on the fact that he was missing "The Simpsons" that he couldn't and wouldn't concentrate, but instead ran about the room, and sank into a corner. This sinking down, from a normally happy, boisterous child, was a sign of some magnitude, so I got him out of the corner and asked him how he felt about tutoring, if he wanted to go on with it, though I really had no intention of letting him escape. It may not actually have been that he wanted to go on, but he certainly didn't want to stop either, and his saying so cheered both of us. I let him go home early so he could see the end of "The Simpsons," and on the way out he gave me a sudden, quite unexpected, and happy hug.

The following week I was up in Boston to visit family over Thanksgiving and went to the Educators Publishing Service in Cambridge, where I'd bought Cox and Cleaver's "Initial Reading Deck" and had been trying it out. My two learners were both familiar with the method, from school apparently, but took to it all the same, so I made a game of it, in which I won the cards they got wrong, they the ones they got right. The element of competition took their fancy, and afterwards they took back the deck to try it out on me. The cards have a picture as well as a letter or phonetic sound on them, and they covered the picture with four fingers, requiring me to supply the word. That gave me an idea for another game, in which we divided up the cards and, covering the picture, guessed in turn. The goal was to help their reading to become more automatic than it had been, though I expect such games are stock in trade elsewhere, and I have the sense of perhaps having reinvented the wheel.

11. Death Comes for a Neighbor

One Sunday morning in December, about 3:00 a.m., a woman from the community was shot to death while dealing drugs by 9th and M St. SW, apparently by another woman whom she knew from prison. There had been a long-standing feud between their families. The slain woman had a daughter in our program, who had been telling people since April that her mother was home, and who, of course, was hit very hard by her death. The funeral was on a Saturday at Holy Redeemer Church, and I was close enough to the daughter to go to it with her tutor and one of the two student leaders of the program, who were also involved.

The woman had been a Catholic, and her funeral mass at Holy Redeemer was a block from the community. Though this is a time for compassion, not judgment, the distant White priest did not warm to the occasion, and as one tutor later remarked, sounded as if he was angry at the woman for having been killed. His sermon reminded us of Christ's love for everyone, though it did so with a certain impersonality ill-suited to the occasion. The barn of a church that held us, the heavy organ music, and the detached tone of his sermon brought no life to the liturgy, but as soon as the last song was over and the priest had all but bolted from the altar, the congregation released its pain. The woman's mother was the first to begin to sob, but nephews and nieces began soon after, and then, as they all slowly made their way out, the mother cried out her daughter's name again and again and again and would not be comforted.

That evening we had the Christmas party for the children in the program, and the little girl whose mother had been killed came to it. Toward the end of the evening, we had the children play musical chairs, and one time when the music stopped, she got into a fight with another child. A tutor quickly plucked them apart and the game went on, but not before the first girl told the other one, "Your aunt killed my mother."

12. Bribery and Corruption

I had been struck, in those very early days, by the realization that phonetic reading, which all our learners had richly encountered at school, was not without its challenges. When one of my learners recovered a word phonetically, he would only retain it if he could get it by heart, which he could only do by seeing it in another context. He could, of course, decode it and sound it out again, but usually, he still did so slowly, and often more reluctantly, the second time through. I couldn't tell how much of this was the learner as opposed to the method. However, at least he seemed to me to have moved on from his September pre-primer level, though whether he would be able to maintain that over Christmas remained to be seen.

Shortly before I left Washington for Christmas I met, on the street and quite by chance, one of my learner's old tutors. She had recently returned from a semester in Czechoslovakia, but was still much concerned with her former student's development. We talked about it and agreed that we would take him on different days, and I began to explain some of the new strategies I would like her to try with him. She was clear and convincing when she described their interaction, like an actor employing a third eye to see him or herself acting.

In the course of our conversation, she remarked that her relationship with Alan had been good until the end, when he realized that she was leaving, and had begun to demand things — mostly candy – as if to rescue something from someone who seemed to be deserting him. Bribery of this kind is not uncommon among the tutors and learners in the program, but I had been resisting it. However, I saw that I should reach out to the tutors again about this, and continued to do so during my whole tenure there.

13. A Barter Economy

A friend sent me a *Washington Post* story I had missed on "food stamp fraud," which described how food stamps are exchanged for drugs. The recipient would get about half the value of the stamps from a dealer, which the dealer in turn would exchange for three-quarters of the value with a store owner or clerk, who would then redeem them at face value. In the course of the story, the writer claimed that the "underground market in food stamps is a thriving business in ... a cluster of mustard-colored brick townhouses that make up the development known as Sursum Corda." The chief informant was a woman who had kids in the program being looked after by their grandmother while the mother was in difficulties. The story passed over in silence the thousands who depend on food stamps to support their children, and of course stirred up more resentment against those who use food stamps by perpetuating the stereotypes that register so often in the pages of the *Post*. But the story also reported that of the 20 million people who receive food stamps, 90 percent are under 18 or over 60, and that the average award per meal is 58 cents; the highest percentage of the participants, 47 percent, are White, with 36 percent Black, 12 Hispanic. The program, which began in 1961, has had an unmistakably good effect on the lives of millions of disadvantaged children. It is widely used in communities like Sursum Corda, where far fewer children go to bed at night hungry because of it, and, needed though it may be, stories like the one in the *Post* do nothing to show its necessity to those who live in the suburbs, nor do they encourage its continuation, let alone its expansion, for those who depend upon it.

14. The City Around Us

I had dinner with David, one of our best tutors, who was involved as a volunteer with the D.C. Fire Department. One incident he described was so unusual that it stuck with me. The
ambulance in which he was assisting arrived first at a domestic fight, which was visible through the window. They waited,
and then a fire engine came, but a small one, so they all waited together. Then came a police car, but not the backup. This
was followed by a second fire engine, probably unnecessarily,
he said, but it was not until the second police car arrived that
the twelve men now assembled went in to stop the fight.

He recalled working another time on a badly wounded
man while five firemen stood around them, facing out, keeping a crowd back. Usually some of their members are Black,
and so they can get a hearing, but often they are simply un-
welcome, and the help they bring is not particularly welcome
either. Domestic disturbances bring them to affluent North
West homes as well, he told me, and they are not particularly
welcome there, either.

David had proven to be a markedly perceptive tutor, and
he said that teaching with us had allowed him to see people more closely than he had before. He knew that he was
welcome with us as he had not been elsewhere in the city. It
was not difficult to understand anger at too large a number of
well-meaning but official helpers, Black and White, he said,
and he credited the community of Sursum Corda itself for our
reception there. He said that it is an honor to work as we do.

15. Loss

A particularly horrible fire broke out in the community during
our early days there. At 8:00 a.m. one morning, it sprang to life
and spread quickly through one of the six-bedroom units on
McKenna Walk, killing three young children aged between

two and four. It was said that a pan on the stove caught fire, and a curtain from that; the apartment was home for sixteen children and three adults. The mother of four of the children had been murdered shortly before Christmas, about six weeks earlier, and there was a general movement to assist the remaining children with clothes, blankets, furniture, and anything else that could help.

The children's problems were such that hardly any of them was skilled in reading, and as a family they now had other difficulties as well. A disinclination to read can have a familial component, and as we have learned from experience, feelings of comradeship can bind together children who don't read well. But why are these difficulties so intractable? There are more things than unwilling children and ineffective teaching strategies involved in what we encountered. The practices of parental enforcement at Sursum Corda are often aimed at control more than encouragement, which is left to the schools. In general, expectations are not high. How can they be? Long before the fire, these children learned that what mattered was survival, not performance, and their mutual love and support, stronger than in many more affluent families, was based on that. Money is produced by social actions that nothing can replace, or so it must have seemed before the fire.

16. Our Learners Knew How to Teach Us

One learner remained a mystery and a challenge. He had one tutor one night, me on another (an unusual arrangement), but he wouldn't believe that he could read, largely because a younger sibling now read much better than he did. He acted up, pretending to read worse than he did so as to disguise it when he couldn't, and even when trying his best, he was not consistent. He said he wanted to be able to read so that when the time came he'd be able to get a driver's license, and though he insisted it wasn't really necessary for that (he claimed to know a driver who couldn't do anything but recognize road signs), he didn't quite believe his own story, and so kept coming.

But he still said, "I'll never be able to read," and said it as though he meant it. Meanwhile, one of the volunteer reading teachers at his school had tested him and had come away saying, "Oh my, he needs help," which, though true, may have been exactly what the boy wanted.

17. A Killing

During all the years that we were at Sursum Corda, I was concerned that the van drivers might hit one of the children who, in spite of our many warnings, would run about as we were, ever so slowly, backing out. Fortunately, thanks to our student drivers, it never happened. On some nights the man who operated the ice cream truck that parked beside the Community Center would keep an eye out, often shouting at a wandering child. But then he was murdered, apparently quite by accident, simply having been in the wrong place at the wrong time, or so it was reported. The police are said to have caught the killers, two young boys, one aged fourteen, the other fifteen, both with automatic weapons. So much of what passes for fact is just information we simply have heard, and not all rumors are borne out.

As I reread what I have written I can see that, for some at least, and not for the first time, I have contributed to a view of Sursum Corda of a violent, lawless community, no place for children, best taken down with the residents evicted, as finally happened in 2017. Sursum Corda's curious Latin name may have helped the *Washington Post* effect the branding of the community that it did, so that the place was effectively stigmatized as dedicated to drugs and crime — a reputation that, once in place, was a real help in allowing those who wanted the land on which it stood to have their way. Also, thanks to that branding, certain incidents that I write about here will seem to confirm the legitimacy of that assault, from which already wealthy White people made more money.

But I cannot say in truth that I was entirely indifferent to its reputation, which added a certain cachet to our work there. Initially, I was chiefly engaged by a program that sought to bring advantaged, usually middle class White students into association with a group of disadvantaged Black children, and I saw from the beginning that the advantages were, or could be, mutual. A Catholic myself, I was further engaged by the circumstance that the connection had come about thanks to a group of Catholic laypersons. They brought some understanding of Catholic social thought into their work, which included the actual construction of the community they then sought to serve. That process seemed somewhat to qualify, if not actually to negate, what some of my colleagues were known to call the "White savior" syndrome, much defamed by those whose interest in social justice is as much theoretical as anything.

The fact that we were teaching reading and the language arts – literacy was, in those days, the preferred word – was enough by itself, and the fact that we acted in a community where violence was not unknown seemed somehow to justify our practices, as long as they were reasonably effective. And we were welcome there. Thus, the greetings we received from those who welcomed us and the general approbation of our work seemed further to confirm our presence there.

But disparities remained, even as we tried to ignore them. We were welcomed, after all, for the children's sake, for the effective teaching we could bring, but, appearances notwithstanding, it was too easy to assume that we were simply friends together, and the conversion of America would begin with us. The echoes of violence, when they sounded, seemed to confirm our moral standing, though of course they did no such thing, and should rather have reminded us how our paths would soon diverge, and the Apartheid that is America would soon rule the fate of many.

Against these hard realities stood what good we tried to do. Occasionally, real friendships between tutors and learners survived graduation, but only rarely. Two tutors married, and they kept in touch with the children they had taught. A third kept her eye on her learner, and very clearly helped him into adulthood. Another returned to Washington years later, found her learner, and became her friend again. And if tutors remembered their learners, learners generally did not forget their tutors either, or often even their lessons. College entrances were few and far between, but they sometimes happened, and even in the course of their days with us, assumptions changed forever, it was said, and sometimes on both sides. The differences that registered, drugs and violence among them, fed, but also changed, a sense of otherness, and left open the possibility that the future might be different from the past, if not for all the nation, then at least for you and me.

Thus, although (*pace* critics) Sursum Corda was by no means innocent of drugs (as are few like communities, especially those that have the bad luck to be situated upon suddenly valuable land), we embraced the community's children, somewhat naively, as loveable in themselves, and as offering an opportunity to cross barriers of race and class without the usual difficulties. We hoped, more than expected, that one day things could be other than they were.

But Sursum Corda was where our learners lived together, with all their siblings, parents, uncles, aunts, grandparents, cousins, friends, and caregivers, and it was where they shared their sometimes painful lives. It was a community that, for all its limitations, gave life and a measure of joy to many of its inhabitants, and had the self-sufficiency not to be beholden to anyone who sought to stare it down. For better and for worse it met life on its own terms, and did so, at least in part, as I have sketched it here.

18. What Changed and Why

I talked to a tutor about the zoo trip, and about his young learner, who had just turned six. He was concerned because of what he called the boy's attitude, swaggering and defiant, particularly when with a friend, thinking that together they could take on all the world. His caregiver did little to mitigate his attitude, and his tutor was concerned that his confidence would lead him only in one direction. He had remonstrated with him, reminded him that he is only six, and sometimes this evoked a moment of reflection -- but not for long.

Later I remembered that the boy was still very much developing, changing as children do during the time they spend with us, and for that reason, among others, we shouldn't jump too fast. It might have been the fact of change his tutor had come upon, since even a perceptive undergraduate can easily be surprised by any change at all in his or her learner and assume it's for the worse. It may have been Gladstone who said that young men assume that not only they themselves, but everything about them will last forever. A senior will generally grant that there's a change between, say, between freshman and junior year, but will take it as the course of nature, nothing that needs comment. But if a student stays in the program two years, he or she may witness changes in his or her learner, and it never fails to surprise when it appears.

19. Race and Reading

Soon after I began working at Sursum Corda, I was engaged with a colleague in examining a thesis on literacy in slave narratives. It recounted a very noble and a very heroic enterprise: an oppressed people's desire to read, and the way they overcame the most extraordinary challenges, all man made, to do so. It seemed to me to give the lie, almost in passing, to the belief that reading is an imposed and not a natural activity. In the course of the discussion concerning his work, I asked the student if he had any experience teaching literacy, because I was struck by the way a number of the accounts reflected stages of development in reading. An example would be the passage in the story of Frederick Douglass's life that I have already mentioned, in which Douglass was taught to read short words of three or four letters by Mrs. Auld. If there is no discrepancy in the account, he then learned to read properly from poor but literate street boys, whom he bribed with bread that was freely available to him at the Auld home. Subsequently, *The Columbian Orator* gave voice to thoughts Douglass had not been able to articulate, partly because of their content, and perhaps too because of their vocabulary.

The accounts of other slaves were not less engaging, with one man learning to read by practicing the letter formations on notes with which he was entrusted, and another learning by noting the words written on pieces of timber during the construction of ships. But in each case, there seem to be the stages familiar to any student of literacy, including the sense of accomplishment and, finally, the satisfaction each account records.

20. The Way We Were

A driver's license still remained our ally. A learner asked to see his tutor's license, and when she showed it to him, asked how she got it. She told him about the test, and he stopped her and asked if you really had to be able to read to take it. When she told him that you did, he said he'd probably never get one then, but she was on to him and told him it depended on how hard he tried.

After hearing this, I was working with a learner, having our next to last meeting of the year. He was in no mood to settle down, but finally managed it, and did a little reading comprehension, which briefly showed him at his best. The week before, we had read some Robert Frost poems together, and, recalling Rilke's description of spring -- "The earth is like a child who knows poems" -- I had tried to see if he would memorize one of the short poems. We settled on "Dust of Snow," four lines printed as eight, which he liked for its brevity and rhyme. On this night a week later, he remembered it, and recited it verbatim as we walked home.

> The way a crow
> Shook down on me
> The dust of snow
> From a hemlock tree
>
> Has given my heart
> A change of mood
> And saved some part
> Of a day I had rued.

We stopped briefly in the parking lot at the head of McKenna Walk where some older boys were playing with a small rubber football, and he caught a long pass in the gathering dusk.

21. Lessons and Opportunities

One spring Sister Roche pointed out to me a clematis which she had planted in the garden in front of the Center as a memorial to one of the children killed in the recent fire. Then she asked me to call by the Office the next Tuesday to talk to a man who would like to donate some word processors, a tricky issue with us, because though the tutors have them and the children love them, I have my doubts, thinking our time is better spent in one-on-one discourse. I said this, and she understood.

We also talked about a recent shooting, the first to take

place within the actual precinct of Sursum Corda in almost a year. It had been absolutely inevitable, she insisted, only a matter of time. She had known well the young man who was murdered, and she'd liked and respected him. He had come out of the military (she wasn't sure which branch) only about a year earlier, and she described having sat and talked with him about his future. He had wanted to leave Sursum Corda and the dubious opportunities it held out, and to use some of his experience and training -- he was fluent in Spanish -- elsewhere. But where were the openings? But then he was drawn into the drug trade, and once involved there, his intelligence and ability enabled him to rise quickly, very quickly, until he was in charge of operations for a large area around Sursum Corda.

Later, I talked to one of our older and more knowing learners about it. He had known the young man in question but was reluctant to say anything much about him. He wasn't surprised the family was moving out, because some of its other members sold drugs too, and they were afraid they might be next. They also were drug users, he added. He listened when I said that that was what drugs bring, and seemed to pay attention to this lesson, though what it meant to him I am not sure. Later, in the van going home, two of the student tutors told me that one of the boys had a beeper, often a sign of helping the drug guys, with him at their tutorial.

22. A Lesson

It was the last meeting with my learner until the following fall. Having known the man who was killed, and the reason, he was more worried about his inability to read, which he feared would someday lead him in that same direction. So, on this day, he applied himself.

We worked well for a while, better than in recent weeks. I remembered meetings with him when I could almost see him growing, moving from word to word, from sight and decoding to reading, from doubt to knowing. The process seemed easy and natural and sure.

But now it was as if there was a wall. I did what I could. I focused on vowels and comprehension. I was encouraging, and for a while it was as if something was happening. But then it faded. He missed words he knew, words he'd gotten right a few minutes earlier. His attention wandered, then vanished. He told me that he couldn't read. He wasn't fooling around, he wasn't laughing now. He looked at the book, then back at me.

He sighed and asked if I would be coming back in September, and I said I would. He nodded and asked if we could stop. I said no, but that I would read to him for a while, and then we could alternate pages. The story was about Julian, from a book he liked, and he agreed. And so, by stages we discovered the rabbits that Julian's father hid in a box for the presentation to his son, and agreed that, after all, it was a pretty good story.

23. First Days

I have been thinking about the first night tutoring, October 3, now many years ago, and recalling what an odd time that had been, and how extraordinary that first tutorial session had seemed to be. But now I do not recall my own reactions so much as the gentle behavior of the boy who became my learner. His mother's boyfriend brought him into the bright, confused downstairs room where we were all meeting, and the boy was none too happy, I thought. He had with him a large arithmetic book, which he put between us like a wall as soon as his guardian left, holding it up to keep me at bay. I knelt down to say hello, to tell him what my name was, and to help to unfasten his jacket, so that he would feel more comfortable.

I remember our looking at each other warily. We went upstairs to work, me carrying the books he had brought. He didn't reveal his nickname until weeks later, and though I recall that we did quite a lot that first night (probably too much: now we tell the tutors to spend the first period simply getting to know their pupil), the effect was probably as great on me as on him.

The next week he forgot to come, and I went to his house to collect him; he (and the man who brought him) didn't forget thereafter. The following night, as we were leaving Georgetown in the van, one of the tutors asked if I would be there all semester if things went badly, and with the hypocritical aplomb of an old hand, I said of course I would.

24. Year's End

Because the body of a young woman had been recently discovered in Rock Creek Park, and it had gotten into the papers, some of the parents didn't allow their children to go on our end-of-semester picnic there. Our group went anyway, allowing others who had signed permission slips along (as usual) to make up for the ones held back. I was struck by how, over the year, my learner had grown. He was now more confident about many things, more sure of himself, physically stronger (he was particularly proud of having stolen second base in a game of stick ball), and also mentally a good deal more perceptive and acute. While we were on the picnic, we went on a walk with two friends of his. One of them was carrying a baseball bat. We were not far along when the boys start asking about wild animals. Then, as if from nowhere, a Great Dane, a really large one with a chain for a collar, suddenly appeared, a small boy's worst imagining, almost as if it had been created by our words. Screams and shouts rang out as the bat was forgotten, and two of the boys and the baffled dog took to their heels, fortunately in different directions.

25. The Lure of Drugs

I have now more details of one of our most painful cases, one I have already mentioned, which involved a six-year-old whose mother was on crack. She had ceased to show much interest in her son, and since the people she associated with used her roughly, she often came back hurt and bruised to the house they shared with her sister and eight others. Her son was confused by all this. He still loved his mother and couldn't understand why people treated her so. But as I noted earlier, he was attracted as well to the physical strength of her new associates and imitated them whenever he could. He was becoming almost aggressively outgoing and even tough. He threw himself into things and didn't care. His aunt tried to do what she could, but he was one of many, and was not hers.

When he was five, he had a good and reasonably close relationship with his tutor, who delighted in it. However, for whatever reason, when he was six, it all broke down. He skipped tutorials, and was attracted to the biggest, strongest man who would pay him attention. One such, a friend -- but not really a friend -- of his mother and in the trade, had told him not to go to tutorials anymore, so for a while he didn't. But then he met his tutor and started to come back. Soon, though, he began missing tutorials again, and skipped the last meeting of the semester. His tutor graduated that year, and I did not know if the boy would agree to continue in the program.

The toll that drugs take is well known to our learners. One evening, I was talking with a learner and his friend when the conversation turned to someone in the community whom they knew, but now distrusted.

"It's always the same," one boy said. "You can tell by the mess in front. If there's anything that should be cut, it never is. And the doorway is never swept. If you can see inside, which is easy to do, the living room's a mess, and you know the rest of the house is too. And the owner has no idea. And doesn't care anyway."

As he spoke, he warmed to the subject, but became angry rather than contemptuous, as if the person of whom he was speaking was not entirely, or at all, to blame for what had come about; rather, the person was having something done to him, something that wasn't fair and wasn't really his fault. Even so, though, the person in question was now best avoided, and would be, by the speaker and his friends.

26. Museum Trip

I had promised to take my learner and a friend of his down to the Mall to have lunch and see the Air and Space Museum the Saturday after our semester had ended, but his friend contracted chicken pox and only my learner came. I don't normally allow individual tutors and students to go on trips without others, but I had promised, so I did it this once.

In the end he liked the semi-educational video games in the museum best, though in one of them he crashed his plane landing on an aircraft carrier too often, and I'm not sure that either of us grasped the principle behind the fusion game even when he finally beat it. Before going there, we had a very good lunch off the hot buffet in the National Gallery, and then went through to the East Building to have a look at some of the twentieth-century art. My learner, who had an open and interested mind, was taken, if briefly, with what we saw, particularly with the room given over to Barnett Newman's *The Stations of the Cross*. We sat in that room, quite alone, for perhaps four minutes. It was a good painting, we decided, but strange. Peaceful, but, as he said, you could feel things.

27. Things Change, but Slowly

Allene Harper, the wonderful woman from the community who, engaged by the university at a modest salary, had given so much direction and support to our program, was attending our graduation to say farewell to our tutors. She and I had lunch together beforehand.

Another murder she said, two nights ago. A White man had come down to buy drugs, but hadn't liked what he had been offered and tried to drive away. He didn't make it. They stopped him, got him out of his car, made him take all his clothes off (probably to get at his money: he was said to have had a thousand dollars), and then shot him dead. Allene was disgusted. Just when things seemed to be getting better, she said, they're not, and she was getting fed up. Then we went to the graduation, and all the students in the program were glad to see her.

A few days later, we talked about the murder again, and now there was a rumor that the victim was an undercover policeman. Allene had been climbing the steps to her sister's house when she'd heard the shots, and had known at once what they were. Suddenly there had been police everywhere. She thought the killers had gotten away, but she wasn't sure. Everybody thought the perpetrators would be caught in the end, that it was only a matter of time.

But she also said that the program, and the student leaders, whom she had come to know well, had changed the way she thought about White people. Before that, she had thought that they really didn't care, or were just talk, but now she saw that at least some do care, and she thought that together we were doing something, changing things for at least some of the little people whom we served.

It was now Memorial Day, so another school year was over. It was so different from the previous year I hardly knew where to begin. More tutors made for a slightly more impersonal program, and we would need to contend with that in the future. On the matter of new books, I wanted to give more attention to pupils who <u>can</u> read and read well. We needed books which would engage, and perhaps non-books as well: magazines, sports stories, and the like. Our drill books never lit up a face, though I think some of our poetry occasionally did.

In some cases, our pupils had little support for their reading from home or even, in one case, from school, and so we had to catch perch with shiners. One of our tutors said a teaspoon of sugar makes the medicine go down, but another countered that we shouldn't identify good books with distasteful medicine.

Chapter 3

Presentations and Performances

1. Berkeley and Back

Because, after two years with our program, I had become aware that all of us in general, and I in particular, needed to know more about the teaching of reading, I spent the first of several summers in California, at the School of Education at Berkeley, taking courses that bore directly on our work at Sursum Corda. These courses showed me the limitations of the approaches we had been using. It was while working in these courses that I became interested in the perspectives and practices of whole language, not only for the possibilities they held out, but also because they seemed to me to address more directly the ability of children to see their world, to understand what is essential and what isn't, and perhaps most important of all, to shape their sense of themselves.

In Berkeley I lived at International House, a large, rambling, Spanish-style student dorm located at the junction of Piedmont and Bancroft just north of the campus. It was built in 1930, much against the wishes of the local residents, who produced a petition against it and issued dire warnings about the inter-racial marriages it would certainly occasion. These duly followed. "I House," as it is universally called, had, even in summer, something of the multi-cultural interplay for which it was known, and, in its cultural diversity, seemed not only open to but also supportive of all persons, programs, and agendas. My room in that first year was on the top floor, with a view of the Golden Gate Bridge which was particularly striking at night. (Subsequently I was not so lucky.) At a reception towards the middle of my time there, I had a conversation with one of the administrators who, in her youth, had been much involved with the Voting Rights movement. She had retained a lively interest in education generally; she certainly knew more than I did about the ins and outs of the Berkeley Education Department, and knew one of the courses I was in. She said she admired it, as I did.

Not all the other students in my classes were primary school teachers. Several taught in secondary or middle schools, and it happened that I came to know some of these best. I had more experience teaching younger children than they did and was not especially troubled to see a young child confuse a *b* with a *d*, or an *m* with an *n*, a circumstance which some of the high school teachers, in particular, seemed to view with dismay. We did some practice teaching at Peralta Primary School in Oakland, and there I was assigned to a gentle and somewhat dreamy eight-year-old boy, who was indeed having difficulty with his reading. He had a particular interest in dinosaurs and in mermaids, which constituted his high-interest material, and which, when supplied by me from the Berkeley Public Library, did the trick. We got on very well together. Not all my colleagues were as fortunate, and I was struck again by the usefulness of our program's connection both to our learners and to their community.

I came away at the end of that summer, as of later ones, not only with a number of new strategies, but also with a better sense of what we might reasonably accomplish. It was in Berkeley, too, that I first read two of Regie Routman's excellent books, *Transitions* (1988) and *Invitations* (1991), with their humane and well-reasoned introduction to whole language teaching. What I found particularly attractive about whole language was its concern to help children become "lifetime readers," not simply functional ones, and its sense that the way to do so is to focus on meaning.

It sounds simple enough, but what it implied was a closer involvement with meaning, and so with value, than the less engaged methodology we had been using, with its emphasis on decoding. Put in those terms, it sounded quite attractive -- who wouldn't want to be more concerned with values? But I was also concerned that, in our program at least, such strategies could produce their own complications, as our students engaged the values and attitudes of their learners. When I wrote some of this in a paper, the teacher reasonably objected that "the Kottmeyer materials (which we then employed) are full of value-laden statements and topics -- *anything* you use will have implied values -- so why not use effective techniques?" And in a whole language classroom, effective techniques and strategies usually mean metacognitive ones that engage the pupil to think and consider, not only to say what is present on the page. "It really is the approach that conveys the message," she wrote again.

Meanwhile, the beginning of the year had not been entirely without incident. When one of our new student-officers went about putting up notices for our first meeting of the old tutors, whom I wished to talk to before they started up again, somebody took them all down. At first, I suspected some bureaucrat who noticed that our posters did not have some requisite stamp or other, but the students insisted that was not the reason, since other unstamped notices had been left undisturbed. I suspected an overreaction, but in any event, it meant we were not be able to start until a few days later. We organized another meeting thereafter, and this was the paper that, in those days, I presented to the returning tutors to get them going again:

Some Things To Try

In engaging and encouraging your pupil, try to remember that there is no one way which will work while all others will fail. Your pupil will probably have certain strategies already, like repeating words before a more difficult word or using visual or syntactic cues to establish context and meaning, and these you should <u>encourage</u>. REMEMBER THAT THE IMPORTANT THING IS TO HELP YOUR PUPIL UNDERSTAND CONTENT, NOT TO READ WORDS IN ISOLATION! You should be flexible and try several approaches each week. Here are some ideas:

1. Rereading: Find a <u>favorite book</u> and have your pupil read and reread it. You may read it the first time to your pupil! Repeated readings especially help with fluency.

2. Writing and drawing: Every meeting! Have your pupil write a sentence (or two or three, depending upon age and ability) and/or draw a picture about the book you have just read. About the hero, or about what happened next, for example. Work on PREDICTION!

3. Sight words! Work on the list provided. Important with beginners, especially.

4. Poems, especially with rhyme and meter, or rhythmic reading. For beginning readers in particular, so as to set up syntactic expectations, but try poetry on all!

5. Cloze: developed in the 1970's, this method requires you to cover a few often-repeated words and have your pupil say, from observing their position and knowing the context, what they are. Sounds odd, but works well. See me if you're not clear what it means.

6. DLTA: Directed Listening-Thinking Activity: You read the story to your pupil, pausing at key moments to ask your pupil to PREDICT what will happen next, based on what has happened so far. Don't react to the prediction, whether right or wrong, but go on with the reading.

7. DRTA: Directed Reading-Thinking Activity: focus on critical thinking: ask your pupil to PREDICT what will happen next, "What do you think will happen?" "Why do you think so?" "How can you prove it?" Important technique!

8. QAR: Question-Answer-Response: this allows your pupil to ask you questions about the reading, and then you to ask your pupil. In turns. Try to establish context, but also to ask interesting, leading questions which go beyond the confines of the text.

9. Write down (in the same notebook you use for your pupil's writing and drawing, but in a separate part), the words missed in reading. Work on them! Be sure your pupil can read them when rereading the book next time.

10. Story Maps. Outline character, setting, problem, goal, events, resolution, consequence, as a way to teach structure. If too complicated: see me.

2. Tutors

Increasingly, if unsurprisingly, what played most directly upon student commitments in an undertaking like ours was the depth and quality of the training, and the extent to which the student tutors knew that they had been effective. If a student-tutor came reasonably well trained and committed to his or her tutoring, then a helpful lesson was likely to follow, after which the student-tutor understood that the learner was indeed gaining ground, and hopefully felt rewarded.

But cases differ, and no two tutors think, act, or react in the same way. Their work with us is only one part of what goes into making them who they are. Many, indeed most, of the students who seek us out have already begun their search for meaning and value, and although it may be that in some cases we precipitate a change of attitude, offer a new direction or even a change of heart, in most we respond to an already existing value rather than initiating a new one. There are exceptions, but for the most part, the making of values is a complex process in which many hands are at work -- hardly ours alone. Still, that is why the quality of the work we do matters as it does. It is not enough that the student-tutor try hard, putting forth his or her best effort -- he or she must be at least reasonably effective, not wasting the learner's time, and taking an interest both in the learner's work and in the learner, too.

Not that our tutors ignore the evident inequalities that their very young charges face; but if that alone is what moves them, they will not remain long in place, since there are so many other, apparently more engaged ways to confront injustices. Whatever else it may be, tutoring also is teaching, and requires the participant to be seriously concerned with the action he or she is performing, not simply with the larger social world which may appear.

Still, in our very early days at Sursum Corda, more than one tutor asked me if working at Sursum Corda would make him a good person. The answer of course was No -- though as I told him, making a stupid joke of it, that it wouldn't make him a bad person, either -- since what he was looking for would come from him, from the sum total of who he was or would become. But it is simply not true that the work we do unfailingly informs -- or improves -- a tutor's values, attitudes, or assumptions, though assumptions seem to me to be what are most often, and most effectively, addressed. But these are the business of the tutor, and no doubt it is possible to carry on more or less unmoved by the world around us, and to let the program become a retreat from the complexities of life. But in my experience, it rarely does. Usually, it is the differences that impress, sometimes forcefully, and rarely does a smart student come away from tutoring unmoved.

If a tutor remains with us for a second semester or a second year, it is usually true that he or she has not only established a good rapport with his or her pupil, but has begun to grow in other ways as well. What most often changes in the tutor, I believe, is what he or she comes to take for granted. Some have no need for any such alteration, and undertake their work knowing full well what they are about and what they mean to accomplish. But sometimes, in talking to a tutor, I became aware that certain words had taken on a different meaning; society will have more people in it; depending upon circumstances, death can have a new edge; work suddenly means work. But the student grows, not necessarily by abandoning old perceptions and prejudices so much as by adding to them, and then by brushing aside the too simple resolutions of the past.

Not that such changes are ours alone. A somewhat conservative student suddenly finds himself teaching in China or in Prague. A more progressive student decides to go on to a graduate school in Education, or apply to Teach for America or the Inner-City Teaching Corps. These are not predictable changes, but they are real enough, and spring from many sources, ours among them.

I said some of this to Lisa, our student director, and she agreed, but added something else. Tutors learn consistency, she said. You've got to be responsible, patient, and dedicated if you're going to make progress. And if you connect with your learner, it's not something you forget. During the time she had been tutoring, her learner certainly had grown, not only by raising his grades, but also by changing his attitude toward school and toward other people. She certainly was one of our most effective tutors.

3. Safety in Numbers

Part of our concern had to do with the physical safety not only of the learners but also of the tutors -- we simply had to have a place of reasonable security for our program to operate effectively. But as we understand the word, safety does not grow out of the barrel of a gun. Because we worked in and for the community, the community offered a measure not only of support, but also of protection. Where violence, by whomever caused, truly rules, the sort of support we provide simply cannot prosper for very long. But we can ally ourselves with those elements in the community that seem to us the most progressive and the most productive, and as they prevail, so do we. It may be that we will lend them some strength as well, but all education relies on other strengths than its own to carry on. In that respect, we are like education everywhere.

4. Langston

My learner and I had been reading and memorizing Langston Hughes, and when it came time to write something for the newsletter I was trying to organize, he offered this, culled from the notes on the author in the back of the book we were reading:

My Favorite Poet

My favorite poet is Langston Hughes. Langston Hughes is the best poet I ever read about. I love Langston Hughes a lot and I wish he never died in 1917. My best poem is Midnight Raffle. The part I like most was the second verse which reads

I lost my nickel
I lost my time
I got back home
Without a dime.

That was the end of it, and when I said it could be longer, he paused for a moment then wrote: "I am glad he got out the ghetto."

The addition surprised me, partly because I had not seen

him use the word ghetto before. I stupidly said that I wasn't sure leaving Joplin, Missouri, and going to Harlem really meant that he was leaving the ghetto, but then I saw what he was telling me, and it was an issue I had been avoiding. A few days before this, a friend and I took my learner and his friend to the zoo, and when the subject had come up as to what other children were writing for the newsletter I said one learner was writing about what he liked about living at Sursum Corda and what he didn't. At once my learner said: "The violence." He paused. "And the killings and shootings." Pause. "And the drugs." He paused again, and I asked what he liked about it. "The houses," he said. "That's one. And friends. That's two." The list continued, and, from what I recall, included his friend's VCR, but not the tutors, who, in spite of all my hinting, he still didn't see as a part of the place, but apart from it. He told me that he didn't want to stay in Sursum Corda, and saw himself as leaving someday, and didn't regret it.

But I had been raised in a different school, and came in believing that community was the key, that this world was and would be a part of his virtues always, which, though different from the ones served up to me, had their own significance.

The learner who wrote the essay had listed this as the first of the reasons for liking Sursum Corda: When the people who shoot people come around, they usually don't shoot children. Another child told his tutor about finding a gun in the street and taking it home, but his father wouldn't let him keep it, and threw it into the river.

Not all the children shared my learner's sense of things. For some, there might as well have been a wall around the place, while others found a warmth there that seemed to offer life. But to a young child there is nothing attractive about violence, except perhaps on TV, and although the sense of community at Sursum Corda, richer as it seemed to me than to my learner, was still present, it could not compensate for everything, or make up for the fear these children felt.

So there was no reason not to do both, to honor those who escaped this hard, fierce place, and also honor those who stayed — or most of them. Let this dear child cast himself as far as he may go, and smelted in the fires about him now, carry his past as a light into his future, without remorse, or doubt, or fear, or longing.

5. Halloween Again

The Halloween season brought the Sursum Corda learners to campus for a party and then trick-or-treating in the dorms. This year they were welcomed into Darnell Hall, long a favorite, and to St. Mary's. The Georgetown students (largely freshmen) who had agreed to take part hung on their door a notice we had supplied, a small orange poster with a pumpkin, so the children would know where to knock. Sometimes the students turned their room into a haunted house or dressed in costumes. Witch costumes were always particularly effective with the nervous Sursum kids, and the year I cite was no exception.

I had followed my learner into Darnell Hall less to watch over him (he went charging ahead and we met at somewhat irregular intervals) than to keep an eye on things generally, and by my presence, to help calm things down. On the third or fourth floor, I saw one room that had been turned into a superbly appointed haunted house, complete with a ghost who stood behind the woman student who was handing out candy. When one of the boys, aged about 10, came up to the room, he was so intent on the chocolate that he completely missed the ghost. The ghost finally leaned forward and said, very gently, "Boo." The boy, suddenly startled, jumped back, but then leapt forward again and hit the ghost quite hard, so that the sheet almost fell off, and the somewhat shaken woman beneath it gave a small cry. I was about to intervene when her roommate took charge, calming things. The boy laughed a little nervously, may even have said a word of apology, and ran on to the next room.

The incident surprised all of us -- the boy too, I think – and though I am not at all sentimental about our learners' recourse to blows, the incident reminded me of a story I had heard a few days before, when on our arrival at Sursum Corda, a certain amount of tension had been evident. The police had come down in force earlier in the evening, and an officer had seen a young man whom he knew from the station house, where there apparently had been a disagreement. The officer took the occasion to remind the young man of their previous meeting in language none too gentle. The young man had responded in kind, and the officer was said to have replied with a blow, which the young man returned, knocking the officer down, according to the report. At once the officer's colleagues intervened, seeking, apparently unsuccessfully, to arrest the young man in question, and pulling their colleague to safety.

The young man would now have to keep an eye open for the "jump outs," as they are called, plain clothes police officers who patrol in unmarked cars and leap out and seize a wanted suspect when they spot him. The "jump outs" are said to come through Sursum Corda on Thursday, though I hardly believe they keep to so regular a schedule. But is it any wonder the boy reacted as he did?

6. Authorship

I was trying to get the tutors to urge their pupils to write more, partly because, in accordance with our practice, it was good for them to do so, and partly because we had promised to supply copy for another issue written by the children of the *Sursum Corda Newsletter*. My learner and I had been reading Langston Hughes' "Theme for English B," and with my encouragement he imitated it thus:

The Theme for English T (Tutoring)
Dedicated to Langston Hughes

My tutor said:
Try to write a page tonight,
and let that page come out of you.
Then it will be true.

I wonder if it's that simple?
I am eleven, Black, born in Washington, D.C.
I went to Walker-Jones, then Holy Trinity.
I am not the only Black student
in the school.

It's not easy to know what is
good or stupid for you or me,
at eleven, my age. Well, I like
to learn,
catch interceptions, catch passes, do math
and computers. I like to do homework,
play games, and draw.

I want a Super Nintendo
for Christmas.
I guess being Black doesn't
make me not like what other folks
and other kids do.

This is part of you, tutor,
you're White --
we're really good friends, that's true.
As I learn from you,
I guess you learn from me --
although I'm Black -- and younger --
and I like to have fun.
This is my page for English T.

I was impressed by the easy way he entered into dialogue with the poem, skipping bits he didn't like, correcting lines that didn't apply, and refusing to engage, at least for now, the subversive rhetoric at the end. But what also struck me was the reference to learning, and perhaps even more, "I like to do homework." But like it he does, at least when we're together, when he seems to find doing it satisfying.

It became clear that Robert Frost and Langston Hughes were the poets my learner, and, as it turned out, several others, liked best. No doubt one of the reasons had to do with meter and rhyme: that was what attracted him to "Midnight Raffle" ("I lost my nickel..."), and to "Stopping by Woods in a Snowy Evening," the two poems he seemed to like best. But there was something else too. In Hughes, he was at once attracted to and yet reluctant about the social themes, and sometimes, as in "Theme for English B," about the political ones, seeing in them something he felt and knew to be true, but didn't yet want to engage, at least not with White me.

7. What Becomes of Tutors

Because I was stopping in New York on my way to a family Thanksgiving in Boston, I arranged to have lunch with two former Sursum tutors now studying at New York University Law School. We were to meet outside the Museum of Modern Art on 53rd Street, which had a Matisse exhibition I wanted to see, but in the end, disliking both crowds and the hassle of getting a ticket, I went to see the Fra Bartolomeo in the Morgan instead. I was reluctant to admit having done so to my friends, whom I had rather chided for not having seen the Matisse, now that they were both New Yorkers. But it gave them the opportunity to say, as we wandered up 5th Avenue, that this was precisely *why* they had not seen it, and to add, which I hardly believed, that students were not particularly welcome in midtown; that was why they had no idea where we should eat.

I had not seen either of them since they'd graduated more than a year ago. In that time, one had taught for a year in China, while the other had engaged in less strenuous occupations. But they were now well into law school, and from what I could tell, seemed to be flourishing. When we came to Trump Tower, I recalled having heard about a cafeteria in the basement, called The Garden Level, and suggested we try it. Once we were inside, though, I allowed them to drag me into the I Tre Merli bistro instead.

It was good to see them and to hear their news, but our conversation soon turned to Sursum Corda. I had brought them greetings from Allene, as well as the latest developments: one young man's former charge had left the program and seemed to be running with a dangerous crowd, but the other's was still persevering. Why did that still matter to them, I wanted to know, and how were their present occupations informed by their previous ones?

It was not a question that was new to them, though I am not sure they welcomed it. They had thought about it in the past, had considered its effects, but recently they had been reading appellate decisions, and what had struck them, even impressed them, was the way, once the trial was over, the "human side" of the case had come to an end. It was then the power of mind and law took over, and while in the past, good had not always come of it, changes had been made, and now, good might. There was danger at such a time, they considered, for allowing personal values any play at all. One had a story that seemed relevant:

A few weeks earlier, there had been a lecture at their law school given by an attorney of some standing who had described, in detail, the ways in which he had achieved his present eminence. In the way of things, he had associated himself with clients whose actions, particularly when directed against the disadvantaged, were simply unscrupulous, and his exposition seemed to some of the students to border on a personal exposé. In the question period that followed, one of the students in the audience had asked him, more or less directly, how he managed to shave in the morning, since that would have involved looking into a mirror, and the question finally provoked a reaction. He had no difficulty at all, thank you, the man had returned, saying he thought the question both rude and naive. In every one of his cases he had been careful, he went on, not to put his own values ahead of those of his client. To do so, he insisted, would have been arrogant, a quality he now discerned in his questioner. It was the duty of the courts to attend to such details, he indicated, not that of the attorney, and his audience would do well to remember it.

My friends were not entirely convinced, but thought there was a point here. They considered that what they had learned at Sursum Corda couldn't apply here, and what's more, didn't, fastened as it was to such a particular time and place. I wondered if that was quite true, and reminded them how "schema theory" indicates that a child's prior knowledge assists him or her in reading, allowing the child to make sense by drawing on what he or she had experienced as well as what had been grasped intuitively or intellectually. One of my friends had read an article recently that had said something of the same thing, maintaining that a judge's background can powerfully color his decisions for good or for bad and influence the way he read the law.

That wasn't exactly what I meant, though I saw the relevance, even for the young men concerned not to misplace values they were still in the process of identifying, wanting neither through fraud nor simple self-deception, to acquiesce in the evident collapse of value they had witnessed. Nor did they wish to impose a still inchoate system where it may have been, strictly speaking, irrelevant. If I understood their position, I wondered if there might not be a kind of middle way between greed and egotism, and quoted, as I had before, Hillel's three questions -- "If I am not for myself, who will be for me? But if I am only for myself, what am I? And if not now, when?" But in all of our talk, I do not believe I said anything that these intrepid young men had not already considered. That night, grinding my slow Amtrak way to Boston, I found in Gabriel Okara's novel *The Voice* this passage, which, not without irony, reminded me of our conversation, and of the law school lessons which neither young man was prepared to swallow:

"'Look, my son, life isn't that way,' the White man started with a quiet teaching voice. 'Life's like playing checkers. If you make the wrong move you are finished. There are some to whom you can tell the truth, however unpleasant, about them to their faces and you get away with it. But the same won't be true of others. They may make things very, very unpleasant for you. See?'"

I thought we might indeed have begun to see, all three of us. Also, we saw that the colonialists' voice, whether in Nigeria or New York, at least for now, seemed to have run its course.

8. Temptation

I had been wondering why one tutor whom I knew well had stopped taking his pupil on any of the Saturday excursions I had been urging, and finally got a chance to ask him about it. It was because of the last one, he said, and what he had been thinking about because of it. This is what he meant:

Claud had been doing well this semester, so Peter had said he would take him, with a friend, anywhere he wanted to go for a Saturday trip. Anywhere. Claud and his friend could choose, though Peter had made a few suggestions: The museums on the Mall? A Georgetown football game? Playing football (or basketball) at Georgetown? A trip to Skyline

Drive? Or even, at a stretch and with others, to the Aquarium in Baltimore? But Claud had a better idea: he wanted to go to Potomac Mills, a huge shopping mall not far from Washington. And he wanted to spend the day there with his friend and Peter's, who was coming too. Peter hesitated; is that all he wanted? Really? Was he sure? Claud was sure. They went.

Afterwards, Peter had had doubts and misgivings. He had given his word, so he had felt he'd had no choice, but it had seemed all wrong. Was that why he had become a tutor: to take a disadvantaged child on a trip to a mall? No radical, he knew how shallow were the pleasures of shopping, of which they had done very little, and disliked having had to abet Claud's self-delusion. He'd felt, too, that consumerism works against the disadvantaged, by giving false images of what constitutes "success," among other reasons, and that to enjoy a trip to a mall was about as big a mistake as 11-year-old Claud could make. But Peter had taken him, even while deciding never again. And no more trips at all, at least not until he had worked this one out.

By the time we spoke, the trip was far enough in the past that we could laugh about it, even though the problem still rankled. We soon got common sense objections out of the way: that he needn't have given in to the undertaking as he did; that he might have altered or added to the conditions; that he had perhaps not yet learned to say "No"; even that Claud was simply drawing on prior knowledge when he made his request, and wanted to visit in person a place he had only heard about before – not a bad thing.

Prior knowledge was the issue in another way as well. We had been talking in my Reading class about schema theory, the idea that children learn to read at least in part by drawing on past experience, on prior knowledge. This worked both for and against Peter's concerns, for on one hand, exposing Claud to the superficial materialism of the mall could indeed dispose him to privilege the goals of the consumer, while on the other, the trip had at least enlarged his frame of reference, and brought him into other associations than those to which he was accustomed. What I could not say to Peter was that his own concerns and influence were likely to be far greater than those of the mall, and that the values which concerned him were as much on offer at Sursum Corda as they are anywhere, so that a trip to a mall seemed to me unlikely to leave a lasting mark. Every house in Sursum Corda had a TV in it, I found myself insisting, and with that the world of glitz and violence that a TV brings. Our children were not innocent of desire, nor did they live in a culture that was so apart as to be free of the constructions that were all around us. Tutors could open doors, but not shut them, and probably shouldn't try.

We talked a little about the "lawnmower" problem, the fact that, since there was not a patch of lawn at Sursum Corda that needed one, we shouldn't use books which had words like "lawnmower" in them, which were obviously intended for a different audience. But the issue was not to teach our kids what "lawnmower" meant (which now they knew anyway from the movie, now on TV, "The Lawnmower Man"), but to create experiences so that their larger world would include words like that one and a million others.

The belief in the absolute separateness of Black and White culture in America is something that seems to me finally regressive and stultifying, and I return to it now because of the context I have just cited. To some Whites it almost seems that the best way to avoid even the imputation of insensitivity in matters of race is to avoid any reference to it. For them, their advantaged backgrounds almost by definition prevent most of them from the ability to interact meaningfully with those whom they tutor. There seems to be an implied assumption not only of economic power, but also of cultural superiority in this deeply mistaken philosophy. There is an easy belief that since interaction infects, the best thing that White people can do is to tend their own exotic gardens, lest they make a cultural wasteland of everything. To be sure, it is not usually inscribed in exactly these terms, but it is not difficult in many universities today to identify those who insist that they are deeply opposed to all forms of exclusion, but who in fact live lives that in some ways exclude. But the truth is that people, like cultures, expand and grow not only by instruction but also by interaction, and in America, the disadvantaged have needs more pressing than the carefully cultivated sensibilities of the economically advantaged.

10. Song

Because our program relied on an association between tutor and learner for part of its effect, I always insisted that tutors never be alone with their learner, even when they would take them to the movies, the museums, or elsewhere, and for the most part I applied the same stricture to myself. At one point I had gone with my learner, his friend, and his friend's tutor, to a children's event at the National Museum of Asian Art, though the friend's tutor had an appointment later in the day, and, stretching the rule, I had agreed to walk them back to Sursum Corda by myself. Wandering up a deserted Saturday afternoon Pennsylvania Avenue, our conversation lagged, but just as we passed the monument the State of Pennsylvania had erected to General George Mead, who had led the Union forces at the battle of Gettysburg, and with nobody about to hear him, my learner's companion felt suddenly liberated and burst into song:

> Glory, glory Hallelujah,
> I hit my teacher with a ruler,
> So she blew me through the door
> With a Colt .44,
> Now there is no me anymore!

Not to be outdone, and after a burst of laughter from all of us, my leaner responded with this Sursum Corda version of "Deck the Halls with Boughs of Holly":

Deck the Halls with gasoline,
Fa la, la, la, la; la, la, la, la.
Light a match and see it gleam,
Fa la, la, la, la; la, la, la, la.
Watch the school burn down to ashes,
Fa la, la, la, la; la, la, la, la.
Aren't you glad you play with matches!
Fa la, la, la, la; la, la, la, la.

But his companion knew yet another song, one, as he later revealed, that he had learned only recently, and that he sang to the tune of "Row, Row, Row, Your Boat:"

Roll, roll, roll your blunt,
Twist it at the end,
Light it up, take a puff,
Pass it to a friend.

But for me that was a bridge too far, and trying very hard not to bring our informal conversation to an end, I did not hesitate to laugh, but also responded as I usually do when the issue of drugs (in any form) presented itself: that drugs are stupid, and that even blunts (legal for adults now in D.C.) do no good at all, but only get you to run with the people who use them and sell them, and who make you do things you otherwise wouldn't, and how once you start you can't stop, even though it looks like fun and easy money at the time. Had I thought that either of these gentle eleven-year-olds was actually involved in the trade I would have taken a somewhat different tack, one that involved "Confrontation and Support," addressing the issue at hand quite directly, while remaining personally supportive and encouraging to the young person being addressed. But I was quite sure they weren't, and so said three things, however problematic they may have sounded to a philosopher: that there is such a thing as right and wrong, that we all know which is which, and that we should do the former, not the latter. I understand that there are those for whom no apology for my remonstrance is required, but a philosopher might have been more conditional, more inclined to stay a judgment so final, so as not to seem morally superior, or to impose cultural uniformity. But I was, as ever, simply (pun intended) concerned for our young learners, not for inculcating transcendental moral absolutes, and felt it important to say to them that right and wrong are not, or certainly are not *always*, products of the moment or the mind, and were not so here and now. I didn't want them to follow my words or my judgments simply because I had said them. Besides, without contradiction, I knew that conditions can alter cases, and no doubt would do so in time to come.

But I wanted them to register that if right and wrong are not simply products of the moment, then sometimes you must act against the grain, if not at first, then finally, to make the choices time lets no one escape. Even so, and thinking that, I tried not to privilege my own experiences and attitudes. Cultural relativism seemed to me, then and there, quite mistaken, and it was certainly not in the best interests of our learners, for whom one wrong choice could end in disaster, leading to the detention center and the hard lessons learned there. At some point these boys might learn a concern for others, but for now, age and circumstance argued against anyone's interests but their own. Also, there were values endorsed by some parts of their community that were simply self-destructive, and among these, attachment to drugs came first of all.

In the end, I agree, enlightened self-interest may not be enough: some children (and adults) live only in their own interests, but somewhat surprisingly, relatively few did at Sursum Corda, where each one had an eye out for the other, in one way or another. What these children knew as right and wrong they learned from many sources: parents, teachers, ministers, tutors, books, stories, experience, reflection. And yet the process of choosing to learn, from whom and when and under what circumstances, was not always expected, and certainly was not always predictable.

In our little program, we usually tried to praise and encourage virtue, rather than to reprehend or challenge vice, for the best of reasons: so as not to sound too grand ourselves, and to avoid condemning anyone's friends or family practices. But if I had said nothing, or had only made a joke as we toiled along Pennsylvania Avenue together, my silence or joke might have seemed to be giving tacit approval to the song's bad assumptions. And if, in time to come, either or both of them were tempted to take a wrong turn, I hoped that perhaps what was once said by someone who cared for them might resonate, and might leave a weight, if only that of a feather, on the right side of the scales. And besides, folk songs have a real force, not only in identifying but also in forming cultural and personal values, so that, little as I like sanctimony, I did not hesitate to have my say. Happily, my intervention did not spoil our afternoon, our unbuttoned mood returned, and we continued on our way.

11. How Tutors Find Their Learners

I had been encouraging my students in an undergraduate course I was teaching for tutors called "Reading, Teaching and Social Reflection" (a title I owe largely to Robert Coles) to reflect upon their experiences in tutoring in their course paper. In varying degrees, most of them did so. One young man provided this account of his first days in our program:

He had met his learner at our Christmas party a year past, but the circumstances had not been auspicious. Twenty minutes after the party began, he heard sounds of a scuffle on the stairwell, and went out to deal with it. There were two boys involved, one he recognized, the other, whose name was Robbie, he did not. The first boy's tutor came up and greeted him, and together, they returned to the party. The second boy's tutor seemed not to be about, and the young man who had broken up the fight spoke to him for a few minutes, then went on his way.

A few minutes later trouble began again, and the same young man went out to the stairs to see what was amiss. This time it was "a bunch of kids wrestling on the edge of the staircase. As I began peeling the kids away from each other, Robbie stood up and almost pushed me down a flight of stairs." Luckily unhurt, he at once turned to Robbie and remonstrated with him.

"Robbie then told me I couldn't lecture him because I was neither his mother nor his tutor," he said. "I replied that it made no difference, that when someone did something wrong, they deserved to be reprimanded. After our little argument, however, Robbie did something that I perceived to be quite strange: he asked me to be his tutor."

The young man said he would, though subsequently he wondered about the wisdom of doing so, agreeing "to tutor a volatile, hostile, and difficult child, who claimed that he had already gone through three tutors." Robbie's family background was really very complex, and the assessment the tutor made was not mistaken. But each young man had seen something in the other which he'd found attractive, and from the beginning each reminded me a little of the other. When the tutor went home, he bought Robbie a Georgetown sweatshirt and t-shirt, and mailed them to him as a Christmas present.

Their early tutorial meetings in the new semester were not particularly happy. The tutor described them as "tests of will," with Robbie refusing to work and the tutor threatening termination, which perhaps did not improve things. Then he had an idea, and he offered Robbie a deal: if he would work hard, for two weeks, the tutor would take him on a trip. Robbie jumped at the chance, and for a while it seemed to work. But then after the trip, which was to an arcade, with a friend, pizza, and a football game thrown in, Robbie returned to his old ways. This time the tutor turned to a cousin, who had some experience tutoring, for advice. His cousin told him to "act like a friend. He also told me I should not only teach him about reading and writing, but about math, astronomy, science, and geography. He suggested I bring a map, or a science book, or a book about the planets every now and again in order to add diversification to our hourly sessions. The greatest advice he gave me, however, was never to give up."

Again, our tutor applied himself, this time with better results. At the same time, he saw one of Robbie's main weakness, the readiness with which he became frustrated and gave up. He showed the boy a video of *Rocky III*, which seemed to actually do some good, but the film was probably only a footnote to his own example. Subsequently too, the tutor employed other strategies: a contract now stipulated that Robbie would "read a book of his choosing (in the event, *Charlotte's Web*, followed by *The Mouse and the Motorcycle*), write a report on the book, and learn to solve complex multiplication and division problems." The number of trips they took together with other tutors and students increased as well.

This was a story that seemed not to end. I saw Robbie off and on during the semester, and concurred with his tutor's modest assessment that within the past year he had "been able to help him a bit." I understood that nothing was promised or forever in what we do, but the happy relationship and the good efforts that emerged seemed to me the result of able and conscientious work from everyone, and to represent a fair part of what our program aimed to accomplish.

12. Communication

We had a number of tutors in the program who were not particularly – or at all – religious, and I tried to be sensitive to
them and to their contribution as I framed my end-of-semester newsletter to the tutors, necessarily alluding both to the
Christmas party we always held, and to what is called Christmas vacation here. In the interests of literacy, I always asked
the tutors to send a Christmas card to their young charges, so
learners would receive a piece of mail addressed to them that
they could read. Christmas was universally celebrated at Sursum Corda, including by a Hindu family whom I knew well,
and it proved no great imposition. Here's the Newsletter.

Sursum Corda Newsletter

Greetings of the season! This will be the last week we will
be tutoring, and our Christmas party, to which parents are invited, will be held on the afternoon of Sunday the 13th. Please
try to come yourself -- it's certainly been a lot of fun in the
past, and should be this year, too. Besides, if the party doesn't
make you want to return to your books nothing will.

It's been a very good semester tutoring, and more or less
on behalf of the university, thank you all very sincerely and
very warmly for the excellent work you have done. I think
most know that this has been the largest number of tutors we
have had in the program, and one result has been a problem
or two -- the learner who moved away and didn't tell anyone;
the other one who didn't really want to be in the program
and so stopped coming; a friend of theirs who didn't want to
work -- but there have been triumphs too, though triumphs in
a tutoring program like ours don't usually make a lot of noise.
But Allene showed me a letter from one of the mothers which
concluded with this P.S.: "Thank you for working with Ash-
ton this year, his first report card is filled with A's and B's." I

suppose it's the parent's pleasure, the child's delight and success in school, and the tutor's engagement which matter more than grades, but it's nice to have them all.

Congratulations to all the tutors who developed, or began to develop, a special relationship with their young learner. You know better than anyone what you have accomplished, and in this season in particular, may you take some satisfaction in it. I hope you have gained from your experience, but I know that you have given much as well, and because of that, the children of Sursum Corda have been well served. Special thanks for coming on those nights when you really didn't want to, when an exam next day, or a Hoya basketball game, or a party with friends seemed every bit as pressing. Quite honestly, your commitment those nights is what best served your child (even if he or she forgot to come), and kept our program green. Warmest thanks to those tutors who had some difficulty with their child, but kept trying, tutoring the assigned child when possible, or whomever wanted to learn when that was not. Our program, after all, is one of those which seeks to address, through the empowerment which education brings, some of the evident inequalities our society has produced, and during this semester I believe we have done what we could. Of course there is more to do, but as Thoreau might say, you have other lives to do it in. May you never altogether leave the program.

Here are three little end of semester hints: 1) Plan for next semester: really think carefully about what you want to accomplish, and do so over Christmas. Bring back a book or two, or a new notebook, and please send a Christmas card to your learner from home. Once the semester starts everything will be a rush, so plan before it begins. Make a fresh start, even if last semester went fine! 2) Patience: actually, most tutors do have quite a lot of this, but if I could find a pill to give us all a little more patience I would get a handful for everyone. Change comes slowly in what we do, but commitment and persistence are at the heart of it. Courage and forward. 3) Learn to say No: particularly when you are out with your learner on a trip, which I remind you is best done in groups of two or three, and with one who knows the turf. But in tutoring as well, in some cases! Be consistent and fair, but final too.

Warmest thanks, good luck on exams, have fun at home and come back soon!

13. How Not to Celebrate Christmas

Three tutors and I had brought a group of six learners from Sursum to Georgetown to play basketball in the Georgetown gym on a Saturday, but now it was time to go home. Stopping by one tutor's apartment on their way to the G-2 bus, the tutor and two of the learners went inside to claim a Christmas present one of the other tutors had left with him, while I waited with the other learners outside. In the apartment, they found, along with the present, a woman friend of theirs who was down from a New York college to visit his roommate.

When they saw the woman in the apartment, I later learned, the older boy, who was about twelve, immediately asked her to teach him to dance. She was standing; there was music playing. But no sooner had she begun to comply than the other learner, a small boy of about ten, put his hands on his hips and suggestively rotated his hips outward, leaving little doubt what he was thinking, however childishly. When his friend saw what he was doing, he fell in with his mood, adding to it by laughing, so that the now irritated woman simply pushed the older boy away, and told him it was time for them to leave. Making what apologies he could, the tutor took the boys out of the apartment.

The boys came out laughing, as from an escapade, and it was not until the tutor spoke to me afterward that I learned what had happened. I made no apology for their behavior, which they knew to be wrong, though both boys had difficult life stories, young as they were. The father of one was murdered, the other's simply left his family. The smaller boy could and did fight with his friends, and when one of the tutors had taken a picture of him on an earlier visit, he tore the camera out of the student's hands and smashed it onto the concrete sidewalk; he said later that he did not know why he had done so. The other boy was less aggressive, but until he met his tutor had had little interest in school or in much of anything. He now valued his relationship with his tutor highly, and yet sometimes appeared to be depressed: on this particular visit he had resented the presence of the other children who seemed to distract his tutor from him, and at one point he temporarily refused to take part in our game.

It did not require the insight of a D. W. Winnicott or a Robert Coles to understand that difficulties ran deep in both these children, and that our efforts were unlikely to answer them fully, if at all. But it still seemed to me mistaken to think that it was impossible to engage them. The effects of association may often be impossible to measure, but our own efforts, however limited their effect might be, did not exist in isolation. As with the extension of school that our teaching sought to offer, so were the simpler social accommodations that we also applied, sometimes unknowingly.

We took the G-2 bus back to Sursum Corda, getting off at Fourth and New Jersey Avenue and walking on from there. Doing so, we passed a bus stop which displayed an advertisement for jeans: a large picture showed a man and a woman, their eyes averted from each other but in a very tight embrace, so that had they not been standing and clothed there would have been no doubt what they were engaged in. "He's having fun," one of the boys said.

It was getting dark by the time we dropped off the last of the learners, and we decided it might not be prudent to return the way we had come, unaccompanied by our learners, whose presence could have supplied a measure of protection. So the tutor and I walked down North Capitol Street to Union Station, and picked up the Metro to Dupont Circle's G-2 bus stop. The escalator was not working, and when we emerged from the hundred-and-twenty step climb into the light, the tutor stopped by a flower stand at the top, and bought, for two dollars, a single pink rose to take back, with more apologies and an explanation, to the woman whom the boys had offended.

14. Lessons Learned

From a student's paper:

"Schema theory ... maintains that a child's ability to comprehend comes from his or her experience with life, and that many reading comprehension problems are ... simply the result of a child's limited exposure to life. My learner and I once read a book that was set at a beach. The text contained words like "dune," "cove" and "inlet," which he stumbled over. Even when I prompted, he would forget the word again, something he usually doesn't do. After we finished the story, we talked about it, and I realized that he had never been to a beach. Together we drew a picture of a beach and labelled things like coves, dunes and inlets. He enjoyed doing so and when I proposed that we read the story again at a later tutoring session, he remembered almost all the words."

Chapter 4

Sabbatical in Britain

1.

This chapter is a departure from what has come before, because it records events that took place when I was on sabbatical from Georgetown years ago, or "study leave," as it used to be called in Britain. During this time, I worked on medieval manuscripts in Oxford, and also spent one day a week, thanks to my time in Berkeley, working as a volunteer reading teacher in a London primary school, learning what I could about urban education in Britain, and admiring much of it. I was warmly welcomed there, and learned far more than I had anticipated, as I hope this account will make clear. I have employed pseudonyms throughout. I end this little prologue by thanking my excellent colleagues in London for their welcome, their instruction, and their example.

I had been in London briefly during August, 1992, partly to arrange details of the visiting fellowship I was to take up the following January at Pembroke College, Oxford, where I had earlier been a student, and whose fellowship had very kindly invited a return. I had called in at the well-known and very impressive Institute of Education in London, to see what I might find out about inner-city primary education in London while pursuing my medieval studies in Oxford. I had the good fortune there to meet a head of department who seemed interested in the work we had been doing at Sursum Corda. I left her with a copy of the account I had written about it, and we talked about the courses in teaching children with reading difficulties and in assessment and evaluation I had taken at Berkeley -- and she kindly invited me to call back when I returned. At the end of January, I did so, and found myself in time for some lectures on spelling, handwriting, and poetry, which I was invited to attend. No doubt part of the reason for the invitation was to look me over and see if I passed muster, but the lectures were interesting and engaging, and my reception left nothing to be desired. The lectures were delivered by a warm and lively lecturer, and though the students were many, I got to know him surprisingly well after class. Spelling and handwriting are not really among my chief delights, but poetry is, and it was in the poetry class we made contact, at least in part by my producing, in the indicated seven minutes, a bit of verse which is unlikely to see the centuries in and out, but which he approved for the effort. During the time I was attending the lectures I had a talk or two with the head of department, who no doubt was looking me over, and who arranged that in February I should visit the Anchorage Primary School, as I shall call it, in Tower Hamlets. I had offered to work on Tuesdays if the Head Teacher wanted it. The alternative was to visit a number of schools in their remit, but reasonably, I think, I preferred one to many.

As I was soon to learn, Anchorage serves a multi-ethnic, but largely Bangladeshi, community located in Tower Hamlets, the borough created in 1965 when three metropolitan boroughs, Bethnal Green, Poplar, and Stepney, were joined together. The 1990 London Docklands Survey reported that Whites made up 65% of Tower Hamlets, Bengalis 22.9%. Other groups it reported included Black Caribbeans who made up 3.6%, Africans, 2.4% and "Other Blacks" 1.1%. Indian, Pakistani, Chinese and "Other Asian" were said to represent 1% each. The White population seems to have greater access to church and private schools than any other part of the community, so that it is the Bangladeshi children who are most represented in the local state schools, and indeed in the area just around the school and north of it, where the percentage of Bangladeshi residents is far higher than in Tower Hamlets as a whole. But in spite of their numbers and mutual associations, the community as a whole could probably not then be described as economically empowered: the same report indicates that although the Bangladeshi community represents 22.9% of the Tower Hamlets population, it represents only 1% of the households owning property there.

When I was working there, the Anchorage School had about 200 students (it has since increased in size), 12 full-time staff and 2 part time, together with a number of Section XI teachers to assist with Bengali -- both writing the language for children and parents (signs in the school are bi-lingual), and also to assist with translation in parent-teacher conferences. When the school first opened, about three-and-a-half years before I joined it, the area had not been notably well served, and in the first year, it enrolled a number of eight, nine, and ten-year-olds who had never been in school before. The children, as the Head Teacher pointed out to me, are usually acquainted with three or more languages: Sylheti (the dialect they use most often in the playground and at home), Bengali (which they learn at home and in community classes), Arabic (which the Muslims among them study in the school they attend from 5:00 to 8:00 three days a week, and which, at this age, many learn to pronounce rather than to read with comprehension), Hindi (gotten primarily from home and from movies), and of course English, their school language. English is the only language in which, from the age of seven, they are tested and judged, though of all the languages it is, for now at least, the one least connected to their lives.

Because school then started at 8:45 A.M. I stayed the night before in North London with some good friends, whose hospitality, advice, and support made my stay a real pleasure. It also gave me Mondays in London, with the opportunity to work on things medieval at the British Library and at the Warburg Institute. It was at the Warburg that I was struck by the linguistic accomplishment of the children, and by the reflection that if any of them, perhaps in a few years' time, held positions at the Warburg, they would indeed be esteemed, not relegated to the bottom of the London tables as Tower Hamlet children sometimes are. But these dear seven-year-olds don't yet have Ph.D.s and don't publish scholarly articles, so their linguistic accomplishments don't compute. Still, and even knowing how ignorant I was of what I was seeking to understand, I found myself wondering about the way Tower Hamlet children were tested. They were being set, as I understood, against groups with which they have so little in common that any comparison seemed to be a travesty of academic measurement. I do not know how British tests are normed, but anyone at all famniliar with inner-city education in America will know what I am alluding to, even though the British schools do not have all the challenges the American schools face.

But I am getting ahead of myself. I began at Anchorage School (again, not its real name) on February 23, less than a month after I arrived in Britain, and after a warm welcome from the Head Teacher (or the Principal, as she would have been designated in the US), an able, perceptive, and energetic woman whose social and educational commitments, I was to learn, were practical and real, the product of many years working in urban education. After a short interview, she introduced me to Lisa Duncan, who had a class of Year 2 children (seven-year-olds, second graders in American). I was to help certain members of her class with reading and as needed. My status was that of "visitor," and it was on that friendly and informal (and, I gather, legally correct) arrangement that I began work. As I was soon to see, Lisa, who taught the class, had the affection and respect of the children, even of the more difficult boys. She also had an M.A., and with it a real sensitivity to her very young charges. Her family, and she herself, were from the East End, though early on she and I discovered mutual associations with Berkeley, where she had worked when her husband was studying there. I also saw early on what an excellent teacher she was, inventive, sensitive, and, as need be, hard-headed.

The classroom was effectively attached to a second classroom, with an open area in between that was used primarily as a materials area; another teacher worked there on projects and filled in as needed elsewhere. There were no fixed desks, but there were work tables for small groups of children, an open area in the middle for class meetings, and an almost separate "home area" behind the front door for role-playing, English conversation, and play. It was certainly a text-rich classroom: all about it there were signs, pictures, and children's drawings, many of the signs in both English and Bengali, the latter contributed by the Section XI teacher who spoke the language and worked part-time in the classroom. There were 28 children in the class, and a slightly smaller number in the class of her friend and colleague who taught in the adjoining classroom. There was also a certain amount of sharing that went on: sharing of materials, ideas, and projects, and the two women planned their weeks together on Tuesday, though each of the classrooms very much had its own identity. Of the 28 children in Lisa's classroom, about 20 had English as a second (or third or fourth) language. In class, they spoke Sylheti naturally among themselves, but, in accordance with the first English objective of the National Curriculum, were encouraged to use English, particularly when playing together in the home area, or when discussing, with peals of laughter, this funny American who had suddenly appeared in their midst.

As I discovered on my second day, multilingualism can lead to complications. Going to comfort one girl who was in tears (she had been pointed out to me by another child, with the clear indication that I should attend to her) I discovered that what was troubling her was the fact that the father of one of her playmates had taken away her family's "felim" and she would never see it again. I tried to be sympathetic, but since I had no idea what a "felim" was, could not help feeling somewhat clueless. "It is a Bangladeshi word," the girl insisted, "you have to know." But in the course of talking it emerged that a felim "goes around," and "you watch it," and after a time I was able to ascertain that, far from being the family treasure I had first imagined, a felim seemed rather to be a video cassette, a "film," and I was able to assure the child that she would certainly see the felim again.

Later, too, one boy, who subsequently became rather attached to me, pulled my sleeve and said what sounded like "To-me-men-tal." When I asked him what it meant he said it meant "You're good," but when I later asked one of my colleagues who spoke Bengali, she laughed and said it meant "You're crazy," so I decided to buy a Bengali-English dictionary without further delay.

2.

I had been reading with some of the children in the morning, partly to try to understand their reading levels, partly to see what I could do to help any who might be having difficulties. As expected, the reading levels varied greatly, with some of the children well advanced, others less so. For whatever reason -- gender fairly obviously played a role -- certain of the boys in the class became very friendly with me, both at playtime, which I sometimes visited, and in class. It emerged that two of them in particular were not very good readers, at least of English. I suggested to Lisa that I could read with each of them, and she agreed. I was interested to see how far sounds influenced their reading, and so I bought two of Dr. Seuss' books, *Fox in Socks* and *The Cat in the Hat*, to see if the boys had any sense of English phonics. *The Cat in the Hat* worked better, largely because its loosely connected narrative gave a sense of order and progression, but they were too advanced for the children I was working with, and I found myself reading to the children, trying to quicken their interest. Both boys lost patience with the wonderfully contrived craziness of *Fox in Socks*, and I wasn't able to interest them in the book's rhyming repetition, which I had hoped might involve them in language, if only for a few pages. Also, there was something of a gap between the two boys, so if I spent time with one, the other became bored. I partly countered this difficulty by getting them to write, which the less able reader did better and more willingly than the other, who only wanted to draw pictures.

We did not work only with Dr. Seuss. I spent a short time as well reading to them, and then getting them to read to me, and with one boy in particular, this last strategy proved useful. Still, for all of this, we did not make a bad beginning, and I resolved to take them separately, and for shorter bursts of time, in the future.

Earlier, I had talked with a part-time teacher who had been telling me about the early days of the school. In the course of our conversation, she said that the difference between primary education in America and in England seemed to her that in America, the more traditional teaching methods were associated with public education, whereas private tended to be more experimental, but in England it was just the opposite. Church schools, whether Anglican or Catholic, tended to be very regimented, she said, with many parents wanting that kind of order, which they thought would be good for their children, making them perform well in tests and so get ahead in life. She had no doubt that we would be getting more tests in the state schools in the future, and that in due course teachers would be judged on how well their children did on those tests. She did not think that this development would be very helpful to many of the country's Bengali children, whose social and educational circumstances are different from those of mainstream middle-class children.

Talking with friends at Oxford about what I was doing in Tower Hamlets, I found that I was very happy with my appointment at Pembroke, a friendly and really quite industrious Oxford college. In those days, the able, famous, and gracious master was the now late Sir Roger Bannister, he of the four-minute mile. He and many of his fellows and junior fellows made me feel most welcome. At least one of the tutors I knew was concerned with encouraging applications from inner-city students, older ones than those I had to do with, and this seemed to me an attractive aspect of the place. But in Britain, as in America, the opening out of education to embrace groups previously excluded or presently on the margins is the crucial task of our century, and the one by which, as institutions, we stand or fall.

3.

I had come to Anchorage for a special assembly to celebrate International Woman's Day, pleased that the Head invited me and impressed at the result. Then afterwards (I had been talking with one of the teachers rather a long time after the assembly was over), the Head asked if I would like to stay on for the afternoon, since one teacher had had an emergency and had to leave, and they could do with another hand just now. I agreed at once. Working in the classroom, however, I had a sense that something was wrong, but put it down to the situation. It was not until the next day, talking to a friend, that I learned what it was.

Late in the prior week, one of the part-time teachers, a man who does drama with the children, had taken one of the more difficult boys out of the parking lot and to his lesson, and when the boy went home that night he had a bloody nose, which he said the teacher had given him. In fact, the teacher and the boy had been alone very briefly, when the alleged (read: utterly invented) "incident" occurred, so that at one brief period, there were no witnesses. In any case, the boy's family had taken the story to one of the school's governors, a man they apparently knew, whom some believed to be no friend of the school, and he had called the police and reported the child's extraordinarily unlikely story, possibly making or implying very serious allegations as he did so. He then organized a petition which charged the teacher with assault, claimed the children were no longer safe in the school, and further objected that the children were shouted at during school lunch. A number of parents signed, and the petition became part of a series of events which quickly unfolded.

There were, as I have indicated, real difficulties with the position of the boy and his family: for one thing, this was the third time he had charged a teacher with something or other, but the last two times there had been witnesses (his stories had many contradictions in any case), and the accounts had been laughed at. This time there was a period when there were no witnesses, though one of the teachers had seen the boy playing quite happily twenty minutes after the incident was said to have occurred and had noted that the boy was in good spirits. Then too, there was a difficulty with the petition: it was not clear whether all the parents had quite understood what they were signing, since some of them do not read English. In particular, it had been signed by one woman who was in charge of overseeing the children at lunchtime. Strictly speaking, she had signed a petition against herself, and when one of the Bengali teachers had asked her why she had done so, she said she thought it was a petition to improve services. Another of the Bengali teachers in the school felt strongly that the petition was a sham, with people signing what they did not understand, simply in order to please the man who had organized it. Meanwhile, the effect of the charges on the career of the teacher in question could be devastating. The charge in the end was not proved (it seemed from the beginning quite impossible that it would be), but the formality of the attack would do nothing for his morale or career. Indeed, why should he stay in the profession?

But a police matter it now was, and when, two days later, we returned from a school trip to Mudchute Farm, an urban farm maintained so that children from London can visit it, certain of the staff had been told that they would be interviewed by the police on the following day. Through all of this, however, I noticed that Lisa had been particularly active in drawing parents into her classroom, urging them to read to the children at the beginning of the day, talking to them after class about the process their children have been making, sometimes with the aid of an interpreter.

Thus, even as events were unfolding, I was impressed by the way in which Lisa and the other teachers continued to engage with the parents, talking to them after school, in not the happiest of circumstances, about their children, taking care that the present circumstances be contained and not strain -- or not further strain -- their relationships. After all, Anchorage was still a very new school, making a way where there was not one before. At least to a degree, it was an outsider in a community, some of whose members believed they had no need for such an addition, at least not so near at hand. Although the events themselves, and the subsequent manipulation of them, were unfortunate, some sort of incident was probably inevitable, if only because of the sort of thing education is. It seemed to me that, perhaps because of its newness, Anchorage was in some sense, as we were at Sursum Corda, on the front line, and if urban children are to be well served -- in arithmetic, language arts and in other social, personal and academic skills -- places like it, responsive to the community but not subject to it, are essential.

But when I returned the following week the situation had improved greatly. Twelve of the twenty-two signers of the petition had taken their names off, insisting that they did not understand the implications of what was written there: few if any of the remaining ten were parents. The father of the boy concerned had written to the school saying that he did not wish to take the matter further as long as the man responsible was dealt with by the Head, but the Head did not believe that the wrong done was the teacher's; it was simply not possible to let the matter drop. Because of the community involvement, the police referred the matter to the Director of Public Prosecution (the DPP) once they had completed their investigation, even while those who precipitated the event had begun to reconsider their action. Other parents wrote letters of support and appreciation to the school, which cheered up everybody. My recollection is that it was expected almost from the beginning that the teacher involved would be cleared and would return to his classes sooner rather than later.

Throughout it all, I was much impressed with my colleagues, most of them women (apart from the young drama teacher in question, whom I never met), and with the tact, good humor, and thoughtfulness they brought to what seemed to me quite an extraordinary situation. Throughout, they displayed, in the face of what some not unreasonably regarded as a particularly unexpected and painful betrayal, a mixture of sensitivity and common sense, conditioned with a marked concern for the children.

I have remembered, retained, and reported the issues here because they seem to me as important as any we deal with in education, even when we discount the personalities and perhaps the prejudices involved. But education is at once a part of, and yet in some sense apart from, any community that it serves. There is a way in which, at least for a time, it does take students away from some part of their parents' world, if only by exposing them to other children – in the United States, this circumstance can cause some parents to embrace home-schooling, I am sorry to say. But in standing somewhat outside the community and, among other things, in bringing children together, it is sometimes necessary that a school, like democracy itself, defend its integrity. The challenges of multi-ethnic teaching, in Washington as in London, in Sursum Corda as at Anchorage School, are many and complex, and involve false starts, bad judgment, and sometimes outright hostility, as well as friendship and support, and that is why I have recounted these events as I have. Teachers are not colonialists (*pace* Freire), and are deeply involved in their learners and their undertaking. Whatever the learner's age, the teacher is in some way seeking, along with education, to help the student discover who he or she is, not simply to mainstream him or her, save in those sad and awful cases that happen in America, when the student is being adapted for a particular role, usually a job at hand, and the teacher is effectively if silently collaborating with the foreman or the manager. That is why, as I say, the events at Anchorage seemed to me as important as any educational challenge that appeared before me in Washington, and it is why I have recorded them here.

Weeks later, the matter I have been describing was resolved. The office of the DPP ruled that there was not a case to answer and dismissed all charges. The young teacher was now free to take up his teaching duties again, though by his own choice, he deferred doing so until the Fall.

While all this had been going on, I was also talking to the Head about an example of prejudice I had heard about from a colleague: on our recent trip to the Natural History Museum in Kensington, one of the guards, who was black, had spoken kindly to one of the boys in our class, who had responded with what sounded to me something like, "kalo bandor." The phrase, I am told, properly pronounced, may mean something like "black monkey." Fortunately, the guard had not understood, but the boy's teacher, fluent in Sylheti, had, and as soon as the man had moved on, remonstrated with the boy. I mentioned the incident to the Head, who sighed, and allowed that the phrase the boy used was not unknown in this community, and added that racism also might have been a factor in the case of the drama teacher, since he was African as well.

Later still, I spoke again to the Head, and this time she questioned my calling it "racism," insisting that "prejudice" would be a better word. She quoted for me a definition in which racism equals prejudice plus power, and pointed out that since the boy (aged 7) was without power, and since he was of course influenced by those about him, it seemed bad manners, if not more, to call him a racist. I understood that the correct sociological term might be "inter-ethnic rivalry," though one of the many unattractive aspects of racism, however named, is the way it turns upon and attacks those who practice it; it is not only its victims who are disadvantaged. The Head understood all this, and of course offered no apology for what was said. But she understood, too, how social constructions carry the seeds of racial division, and given the role of economic difference, knew how varied the effects of these divisions would come to be in time. Perhaps so, but in America, as at Anchorage School, it seemed to me that in a way racism is like power: it has many faces, though at heart they are all one, and when all is said and done, youth can be but one of them.

Then it was suddenly the end of the year at Anchorage, and this happened: a number of White parents (five, as I recall) give notice that they were going to withdraw their children from Anchorage and enroll them in the Church of England school not far away. I heard one of the mothers tell her child's teacher: "Don't take it personally, it's not you at all." But we all knew it was not: the teacher is White. I went to lunch with her and with her friend, who taught in the adjoining classroom, and we discussed the situation. They had a certain sympathy for the Head at the Church of England school, who was not thought to be in the least racist, and they speculated that the parents may have found a way around her, perhaps through the Board of Governors, if there was one. In these circumstances, the claim "I want my child to have a Christian education," was sometimes code for "I don't want my child to be in class with Bangladeshi children, or at least not too many of them." I was told that if the Head of a church school (whether Church of England, Catholic or other) saw the request for what it was, he or she could sometimes find a way out: racist parents are not often regular church-goers, and sometimes that circumstance can be employed, or the class can simply be declared full. But most schools here (private ones, called public schools, apart) are in one way or another state schools, even, to my surprise, if they are affiliated with a church. There is pressure on them to add students, particularly now that the amount of money the state pays to each school depends on the number of children it enrolls -- disadvantaging teachers' salaries, among other things, since experienced teachers cost a school a greater percentage of its budget than new graduates. Under these circumstances, it is not difficult to imagine a time when a Head might not inquire too closely about the reasons for a new student's seeking admission, though that seems not to have been the case here.

Still, real world problems are rarely metaphysical, or at least not only so. When parents take their children to Bangladesh for five or six months, so disrupting their education, not all Heads are willing and able to take them back when they return, though my companions estimated that state schools are more likely to do so than church ones. Of course, all children have a right to an education here, and I am told that there is an office somewhere that can inform parents which schools have spaces in them. But here, as in America, there are marginalized groups that are unable, to use an American phrase, to hassle the bureaucracy, and as we discussed these things I began to understand why, when Anchorage was first opened, eight, nine, and even ten-year-old children were said to have been found in the neighborhood who had not been to school a day in their lives.

5.

Singing has an honored place in the curriculum here, though I was a little surprised to hear the American Civil War song "John Brown's Body," reborn as "John Brown's Baby," who is said to have "a cold upon his chest," which will require treatment by "camphorated oil."   But the children also celebrate the end of Ramadan by singing "Khusir Idd" ("A Happy Eid"), which many of them already know, and "Hot Cross Buns" in acknowledgment of Good Friday.

Eid is the feast with which Ramadan concludes, and takes place twice a year; this is the lesser of the two celebrations, though much enjoyed by everyone. But it seemed somehow appropriate that Ramadan, a moveable feast associated with the moon, should fall in March that year, since this was the month of the National Curriculum Science Test. The tests for seven-year-olds came relatively early in the year, and had now been largely completed. As a result, they were not caught up in court and union actions as the tests for older children had been.

Toward the beginning of the year, all the relevant teachers had received a letter from the Ministry of Education that certainly sounded as though it was meant to intimidate, though in fact it only urged that all teachers had a contractual duty to administer the test. But that was precisely the point that the unions took up when they brought the matter to court, insisting, I am told, that they had a legal right to boycott the tests since they called for a good deal of work not contracted for, work over and above what had been agreed upon, and the court sustained their objection.

I remember being surprised by this approach, since it seemed to me apparent that the real difficulty with the tests is that they are said not to have been normed on children like ours, and so were inappropriate for them. From what I heard repeatedly, they were introduced without appropriate consultation, and in such a way that, it was said, crediting the results might do as much harm as good. It was notable that the one borough which warmly supported the tests was believed by the teachers with whom I spoke to be one of the richest, where the children seemed to have certain social and academic advantages, and it was suggested that those supporting the tests had calculated that it may have been in the best interests of their children to do so. The line they took was that their children had been preparing for the tests for some years and they did not wish to disappoint them, so they hired supply teachers to administer the tests, a practice that one union representative approved. But it was almost as though, in American terms for a moment, certain schools in wealthier boroughs had become "magnet schools" (but ones not open to all children), and that the great advantage of a school system that seeks to serve all children equally may have been impaired. All too often, this certainly has been the American experience. There may, of course, be ways to address this problem, but to do so requires cooperation and consultation, and they seemed, in this case at least, to be in short supply. I found myself curious to know why they were refused, since the establishment of the national curriculum as it then came about by the same kind of consultation and compromise for which the present situation seemed to cry out.

Somewhat unreasonably, I was particularly surprised by what seemed to be the official attitude because of the very favorable impression I had formed of Mr. John Patten, formerly the Member of Parliament, or M.P., for Oxford (there was only one in those days), some years ago when I met him, quite by chance. I had been working in Bodley, then the main Oxford University library, and had gone for a morning coffee to the King's Arms, when I saw there a friend sitting at a table with a young couple whom I did not know. I joined them. Introductions having been made, I was told that they were waiting for John Patten, who had arranged to meet the couple to tell them what he was doing to help an Indian friend of theirs, already living in Britain, who was having some difficulty with immigration.

I recall being taken aback by the idea that their M.P. (a former geography don at Hertford, as I knew) was going to meet them in a pub -- not a place an American politician would readily appear to consult with a constituent -- and wondered for a moment if this could be a version of that old parlor game "Putting the Yank On," -- next week, let's see if we can get him to believe the Prime Minister is coming, and the week after that, the Queen. That unworthy doubt returns to me as I write this, though even then I thought that circumstances were against it.

In any event, in due course a youngish man who certainly said he was John Patten appeared, courteously declined the cup of coffee he was offered, and explained, in what I recall as informed detail, the circumstances of the case, where things stood and what he could, and would, do to help her case. I remember being really impressed at his evident understanding of what was at issue, and also, to tell the truth, that he would come into this place, meet two constituents who were hardly local power-brokers, and explain the details of a case from which he had little to gain, but in which he (not only his staff) had evidently taken an interest. I never learned what finally happened to the application -- when I asked my friend later he either didn't know or the matter had not yet been resolved -- but the image of an able, intelligent, and responsive M.P. stayed with me, and later on, when I heard that he had been caught up in some complicated business, I felt a certain sympathy for him, and hoped that as with the case at the school, in the end all would be well.

But when I finally saw one part of the test it seemed to me that the unions and the courts were probably quite right: it simply would require a real effort to give the tests properly, and doing so would mean that time must be taken away from lessons, which would be effectively lost, as happens in America. The test is administered to each child individually; the questions are read to him or her and the answer given was recorded. While this was going on the class was meant to be getting on with its work, though this would have proved all but impossible given the concentration the tests required. When the teacher first told the children about the tests they became nervous, but she did everything she could to reassure and support them -- "Of course you can do it, it's easy" -- and her encouragement seems to have had its effect, as many of the children certainly made a good show. But the testing, which was a real strain, did take her away from teaching, and looking at the thing as a whole, I had the sense it was not the better part of wisdom to lay this sort of thing on seven-year-olds.

6.

Referring to my early work at Anchorage, I wrote rather flippantly that one difficulty the children faced was that they did not have Ph.D.s, nor did they publish academic articles, so their reading and linguistic abilities were undervalued. After that, I worked with three or four children on their reading rather closely, mostly those whose reading their teacher was concerned about, but also a few others, and I began to get a good idea as to how they proceeded. I have already mentioned that I was surprised how little the children used phonics, or were disposed to use it, even when I very briefly sought to introduce it as a strategy. The idea that letters make sounds was not new to them, and with a few letters (vowels more than consonants, to my surprise) they had a sense of what the sounds might be, but there was certainly no inclination to move ahead. What there was instead was a reliance on sight and on memory. With these came none of the usual strategies. There was no repetition of words preceding an unfamiliar word to establish syntactic context, no sense, from what I could tell, of *any* syntactic strategy. Instead, the learner would simply jump to the next word he or she recognized, with no inclination to supply syntax or meaning for whatever came in between. Thus, the reader seemed to take the identification of words as the point of the exercise. There was a *very* limited use of context cues in previewing what might be in the book or in predicting what was to happen, but even these strategies, which I sought to encourage, seemed to me to have derived, when practiced, from other books, hardly at all from experience. Indeed, when the boys came to me -- I knew them all well by the time we had been worked out what I was to do -- they came clutching the most elementary of texts, ones they had effectively memorized, and it was not easy to move them on to other books, though once we shifted to one-on-one, things became easier. The term "favorite books" in this context took on a special meaning, and for the boys I was working with, even "choosing" meant, as it often does, a sort of process of elimination, not an engagement of the heart.

What struck me as I conducted these lessons was the way the limitations of my approach were in some way related to the multi-ethnic, and particularly multilingual, community in which these children lived. Theirs was a world rich in culture, but that richness could impose a limitation, for some at least, on their ability to read and write in English. The distrust of sound and of context was entirely understandable in children for whom similar or identical graphemes could produce entirely different phonemes, and in syntactic constructions that could prove radically different. The only thing to trust was what you could see and remember. Words, or at least the letters that produced them, appear fixed, should mean one thing, and ought never to change. But sometimes they did. Thus, the grapheme/phoneme relationship was not at all meaningless, but it was insecure. Thanks in no small part, I came to consider, to the number of languages involved, identical graphemes could regularly and sometimes unaccountably produce different phonemes.

Put in these terms, the conclusions seemed obvious enough, but I did not understand what was happening until I worked with a boy who read very well (how well I did not know at the time). In the course of our work, we came upon a word he didn't know. We were not in the somewhat enclosed but still transparent "home area" where I usually worked, but were over by the window on the side wall. From there, he could see out the back windows as well and into the schoolyard, so that at first, I thought he had been distracted by something he had seen going on outside.

"Come on, pay attention," I said. "Stop and think. What do you think it means?"

"I don't know. I don't know it."

I tried again. "Look what's happening. What do you think it means?"

No good. He just stopped and seemed to have no back-up strategy at all. It was only then that, as the British say, the coin dropped, and I finally understood what I was looking at, and indeed had been looking at for some weeks. This excellent child (and able reader) had no more strategies at his disposal than his less literate classmates, only a better memory, and a greater willingness to use it to guess, and so to put it at the disposal of his reading. I caught myself, gave him the word, and we moved on.

Partly to ensure that I had understood what seemed to me to be happening, partly out of simple curiosity, I worked with several students whom I knew to be good readers and looked for a common denominator. They were, of course, as different from one another as it was possible to be, but they had two things in common: they were read to in English from their earliest years, and they had seen an authority figure in their home, usually a mother, sometimes a father or an older sibling, read books, often in more than one language. One very able boy took a real pride in his accomplishment of being able to read in Bengali, in Arabic (the alphabet and some words), and in English. But in the present system, only one of these mattered.

Throughout, I had the sense that the variety of cultures about these children could put some of them, if only temporarily, at a disadvantage, making their class work more difficult, not easier. I knew that in the United States ESL (English as a Second Language) children can develop the same strategies as their monolingual classmates, but for the most part, American ESL children have only one other language to contend with, not two or three or four. The greater the number of languages, the more difficult it seems to be to employ the very strategies which are needed to contend with English.

When I talked about all this with my fellow teachers, they agreed, and pointed out to me that since the children concerned regularly speak in both Bengali and Sylheti, among other languages, they often would come upon words that can have two quite different pronunciations, but mean exactly the same thing. They probably would only read texts written in Bengali, which they might also speak, but knowing the Sylheti dialect as well, could assume that the same graphemes might represent two entirely different phonemes -- a circumstance that would induce no confidence, at least at their age, that things are any better in English. In English, after all, only twenty-six graphemes (the letters of the alphabet) are employed to represent forty-four phonemes (the basic sounds of English).

It was with this understanding in mind that I subsequently tried an exercise I had learned at Berkeley called "phonemic segmentation" with the boy in question. I wanted to see if, by focusing upon an ability to "count" English phonemes, I could induce in him some confidence in the grapheme/phoneme relationship, but my recollection is that it was too late in my time there to really determine an outcome.

Still, I came away from my experience with the sense that the linguistic circumstances in which the children I had been teaching lived had the possibility of depriving some of them of certain strategies that other children enjoyed, and might even have initially limited the ways in which they could address whatever text came before them.

I understood that this limitation could also be an advantage, linking the children to more languages, texts, and cultures than their more middle-class counterparts. Indeed, their circumstances made me see much more clearly than before how language is at the heart of the multi-cultural argument that is now so current in America: language, sometimes a wing, sometimes a ball and chain, certainly does seem to be at the heart of any culture, a fact which the more superficial discussions of multi-culturalism often pass over in silence.

In the case of these children, the new tests that were being prepared would measure them against a norm fixed for students living in different social circumstances, students who were not necessarily brighter or in any way "better," but whose familial and other circumstances were better attuned to what would be required of them. And the valuation which would fall on them might follow them – for how long a time I have no idea. This seemed to me a pity, and also a mistake, since this new Britain that we were living in was more of a multi-cultural country than it ever had been, and that fact should have been a source of strength, not division.

But I had to do with these children, not those attitudes, and, as before, came to consider that one thing that might help in these circumstances was writing.

So I adapted the sort of one-on-one tutorial arrangement that we used at Sursum Corda and that I had used before at

Anchorage. It gave practice in addressing individual and unfamiliar words, imagining and understanding context, focusing attention, and what seemed to me most important, constructing meaning. But it was early days yet, and I did not mean to offer writing as a panacea for such a complex problem, one that I myself had only just begun to understand.

I know that among the objections that could be posed to what I have written is that I have had to do with very few pupils -- so few, in fact, I would be reluctant to call them a sample -- and that they were, for the most part, selected because they had reading difficulties that most of their classmates did not. Their difficulties may have been more localized than I have been suggesting and might owe more to nurture than to nature.

But I believe that what I observed was far from incidental. It certainly did not seem to me to have been simply anecdotal, and the extreme youth of the children involved seemed to support this inquiry, which I offer more as a product of pedagogical than of theoretical observation. It may be that at a slightly later age the distinctions between and among languages becomes less difficult, particularly as the learners' experience of spoken English increases, and any residual difficulties, if they still exist, both decrease and escape notice.

But it may be possible that the observation could at least provide an opportunity for further research, and then might also offer the possibility of identifying a teaching strategy to address it. To this possibility I can only add that the lines I saw drawn, though admittedly few in number and among very young children, seemed to me so sharp as to be unmistakable, the reactions so unguarded that I do not believe I was deceived. The simple truth is that there was nothing outlandish in any of this, and what I have described is about as unfamiliar as the wheel to those who work with these learners. Multi-lingual children are placed at a disadvantage, not because of any intellectual, cultural, or personal limitation of

their own, but because of the social and pedagogical structures around them. Those structures are directed at another
group of children altogether, and do not always take into account the different ways and rates of development of the children I had to do with, or the different drummer to which they
must surely have marched.

7.

I have had occasion to mention the energetic and very capable materials area teacher who worked between the two classrooms and whom I met on my first day at Anchorage. What
I did not write before was that our first meeting could not really be described as altogether happy. In the afternoon of that
day, the class in the attached classroom was away on a school
trip to Mudchute Farm, (which I have already mentioned, and
which we visited later), and the homeroom teacher had gone
with them to help with supervision. But as it turned out, the
other teacher who was usually present had to be away from
school that day, and when the time came for her to leave, the
first teacher had not yet returned, so that I was left in charge. I
was, of course, somewhat nonplussed with the arrangement,
but it was good being with the children on my own, as it were,
and things certainly seemed to go well.

In something over an hour, the missing class returned, and
both teachers with them. At that point, the day was almost
over, the children were out at their final recess, and I had gone
out as well to be with them, to keep an eye on things. What
I had not noticed was that three pupils had remained in the
classroom. The other teacher spotted me in the schoolyard.
We had not yet met, but she evidently took me for a supply
teacher, and she came out to inform me about the children
inside, with the implication that I had left them unsupervised.
I repaired to the classroom so they should not be alone any
longer. For the final assembly, I wanted to do some choral

reading from one of the big books, but as I was preparing to do so, she asked me, in a tone that was hardly encouraging, when, precisely, I meant to mark the register.

"The register?" I inquired. She gave me a look which suggested that it must be only with the greatest difficulty that I was able to find my way to work. "The register," she repeated, and showed me where it lay. I took the roll and turned to a big book called *Meanies*.

When we talked again the following week, she had become welcoming and friendly. She regretted we had met on the terms we had -- she had indeed taken me for a not overly clever supply teacher. We talked about things, and as we did so I began to appreciate her position, poised as it was between two classrooms. She took part in the planning and running of the classes, but less so in their organization, and had more often to administer direction than give it. That being the case, she could not fail to represent and defend her own position when it became necessary to do so. She planned to apply to take over one of the classes in the next year or soon thereafter, if a place came free.

She was also one of the two non-Asians in the school who spoke Sylheti, and who had visited Sylhet, where she stayed one night on a trip to the sub-continent. In a way, this was a sensitive point, since it was the official policy to encourage the children to speak English while they were in school. Even Section XI teachers, who spoke both whatever dialect may be useful and English, were intended only to facilitate communication between teachers, administrators, and parents, and to provide a cultural and linguistic bridge for the children. But later, on a school trip to Mudchute Farm, I heard the children ask her the English meaning of certain Bengali words. Her language skill was also a help when I saw that some of the children were having difficulty in a Dr. Seuss book with the English word "tall," for which there is no exact Bengali equivalent, so that the children were inclined to use the word for "long" instead.

Meanwhile, the school had voted to support the boycott, so that the staff would not have to complete the tests that had begun, and the whole process came to an end. Anchorage had a wide range of political opinions among its staff, but the decision was easily reached, even by the more conservative teachers. There is really not too much to write about this matter. Everyone concerned believed it to be a bad test, unfair to the children, and that it would be wrong, both professionally and on a more personal level, for teachers to administer it. My own sense was that they were not mistaken, and I remember being surprised that the government had persisted. Really, the point seemed to me that Tower Hamlets' children are as British as the dons in Oxford. But any national measurement must somehow be fair for one and all.

8.

I tried again, in what I fondly believed to be the best interests of my students, to mix comprehension with phonics, this time using Dr. Seuss' *Hop on Pop*, the simplest phonics book I could find at Blackwell's Children's Shop, which, understandably, was not very well supplied with books able to engage urban and ethnic minority children. I was working with both the second year and third year classes at that point, and the book worked well enough for those children who only read English. However, those who were bi- or tri-lingual were still at sea.

The book pairs a number of words in which the change of the first letter changes the word -- hop/pop, house/mouse, and so on -- and I was struck again at the way the children resisted both visual and phonetic cues (the book hardly allows for syntactic ones), and although "house" came easily, "mouse," even with prompting, did not. I still had the sense that what I was looking at was the product, at least in part, of the influence of several languages, and also that there was more to all this than I had imagined. The knot would not be cut so easily.

For one thing, it was clear that syntax was not less important than sound, but beyond that, the difficulty of working with a book as innocent of plot as *Hop on Pop* makes its own problems and limits the engagement of those for whom language already is a problem. One of the children who easily read *Hop on Pop* objected to its evident lack of structure, though another read it to the end. But when all was said and done, I was struck again, and more forcibly, at the evident disparity between the groups, and by the ways in which some of the children lacked certain strategies at least in part because of the circumstances of their lives.

The class topic this term had been "Living Things," and at the planning session one day, the teacher told her colleagues a story (which I expect happened at another school) concerning the death of the class hamster. The teacher in charge used the occasion to discuss death with his class, and a good discussion followed, after which teacher and class buried the hamster with some ceremony in the school grounds. But when the teacher told the story in the Staff Room after school, somebody thought he remembered that hamsters hibernate. They all rushed down to the grave and exhumed the poor beast, who still looked dead as he could be. Someone tried to massage its heart. No success. Then someone else recalled a time when a drop of sherry served to revive him: a bottle of sherry and an eyedropper were produced and employed, again without result. At this point eyes began to meet, recognition arrived, and the poor thing was decently reinterred.

9.

I had been working with the children for some weeks, and though I hesitate to describe what I had come up with as a system, it worked somewhat like this: first, I tried to work out a different strategy for each of the children. It had taken on a rather extreme form, since in one case I no longer called the child in to read with me, but rather let him decide when he wanted to read. The only thing was that he could not interrupt the lesson of another child, but had to ask to come in afterwards. I should say that I usually worked in the "home area," an enclosed but easily visible part of the classroom designed for play. It had the advantage of letting all the children see what was going on, while providing a somewhat enclosed area that encouraged concentration. On the other hand, it also had the disadvantage of monopolizing a play area which, alas, sometimes had to be defended against children who wanted to use it for play.

Within the lesson, I used primarily comprehension strategies, though often mixing them with Dr. Seuss books (*Hop on Pop*, sometimes some pages from *The Cat in the Hat*), as much for the narrative as for anything. When a child showed a strength of any sort, I built toward it, but even then, I tried to focus attention on meaning by using previewing and predicting strategies.

I had a piquant moment one day when one boy, who was just getting on with his reading for the first time, said "Don't." And then, "Be quiet," when I sought to interrupt the flow of words that suddenly, and for the first time in his life, was gushing from him. And when I again sought, a minute later, to see if he understood what he was reading, he said, "I said be quiet."

But reading is not simply the ability to recover words from a page or working out what's printed on a bit of paper. In the beginning, the children were reluctant to make any use at all of prior knowledge, except perhaps what they had found in other books, and that limited their willingness to work with much zest. That changed in due course, so that children who had no difficulty in reading wanted to come in for a lesson, and it was difficult to say no, since by their request they supported the value and importance of reading. It also gave a kind of nudge to those who didn't -- besides, it was good to be able to hear how well they were doing as a point of comparison with my "regulars."

10.

Once, while I was in the middle of things, I heard one of the classroom teachers remonstrating with a Section XI teacher about some work she had overseen. The classroom teacher had left an example of some writing and drawing as the sort of thing she wanted the children to do, and the Section XI teacher had made the children copy the example carefully, paying particular attention to handwriting, and reproducing accurately what she had taken to be an exemplar.

But for the classroom teacher the example was just that, and the last thing she wanted was what, to her, was simple imitation, though she accepted that her directions may have lacked clarity. Later, I talked with the teacher, who had no training in primary education and reasonably understood her position to be concerned mostly with translating and interpreting. However, she now understood what the issue was, though understandably felt somewhat hard done by. We agreed that translating and interpreting were indeed important to the school and that it had been a long day for both of us.

Later that day, one of the boys I work with delighted me by explaining that I should come on Monday and Wednesday as well as Tuesday, and in fact that I should come every day. When I tried to explain something about having to do other work at libraries, he said that that made no difference at all, since there was a library in the school and I could work there when I had to.

11.

But now suddenly it was 2017, and thanks to a news article on page A14 of the October 11 *Washington Post,* I was able to find on the internet a report I came to admire very much: *Healing a Divided Britain: The Need for a Comprehensive Race Equality Strategy,* published by the (British) Equality and Human Rights Commission. Intended for policy makers and others, it methodically and thoughtfully examines not only "the key challenges to race equality in Britain," but also presents the evidence for its findings and recommendations, in matters relating to education; work, income and the economy; health care; justice, security and the right to life, all within the context of the connections that exist, or should, between the individual and society. It pulls no punches, graphically reminding its readers that "Race remains the most commonly recorded motivation for hate crimes in England and Wales at 82%."

But its focus throughout is what we in America would call positive, even restorative, and while the document is so rich that I cannot summarize it here, reading it, I was struck by the ways in which justice and the economy so powerfully interact. These, it seems to me, must claim a precedence, even over health and, dare I say it, education, in any new attempt to right the scales.

I recall once a colleague citing Danton (of all people!) saying that, after bread, what the people most need is education, and in France's revolutionary period such may have been the case. But now, at least, without a fair measure of legal and economic justice, even education is too soon at a loss, at best preaching or predicting a way for some, not all. Reading this perceptive little text, I was reminded of so much that I have written here, and what struck me, again and again, were echoes of our work at Sursum Corda. I found myself wishing that a similar American body would produce a like report – concise, detailed, and to the point, both recounting a troubled past and a painful present (though those reported in England may not be as troubled as our own), while also holding out the possibility of something better, something within reach. The Equality and Human Rights Commission represents itself as promoting and enforcing "the laws that protect fairness, dignity and respect," and issuing "periodic reports," of which this was one.

12.

Toward the end of my sabbatical, I found on the open shelves in the British Library a fair account of Tower Hamlets itself. Though the borough was formed as late as 1965, its name is far older, having been first indicated in 1554, when the Council "ordered a muster of the men of the hamlets 'which owe their services to the Tower'," and formalized in 1605, when East London "was made a distinct military unity with the official name of 'Tower Hamlets'." By 1684, those who lived there were described as "'generally very factious and poor'."

But even these indications suggested a place contained by stricture and raided for men, a place described rather than defined, observed rather than held. Even the presence of the thoughtless rich among them (Charles I once killed a deer among what are now the housing estates) could not scatter the inhabitants, who remained not quite contained, somewhat disadvantaged, and stubbornly present, a standing judgment on the world beyond the Tower.

As I have said before, I have had to do with the children, and have seen their community refracted in their eyes, human and warm and filled with contradictions, intimately a part of and yet also apart from the school that touches nearest to its heart. I had come here to learn more about the ways urban schools address their youngest children, and thanks to our Head, to my colleagues, and to the children themselves, I was not disappointed.

But I had been reminded too that education is a mystery, and we move among forces we understand only in part. Tower Hamlets was no great distance from Sursum Corda, nor Sylhet from Washington. Some journeys never end.

Chapter 5

Sursum Corda If You Can

My engagement with Anchorage School, as I have been calling it, seemed to end when I left it in 1993 – I received a very friendly but semi-formal farewell, complete with presents -- a card signed and inscribed by my colleagues, paperback books, and a video called "Culloden," concerning a so-named Tower Hamlets school that had allowed the BBC to film its operations over the course of an academic year, and that I subsequently used in one of my Georgetown courses.

But then I returned to Oxford seven years later, in 2000, having received the Keeley Visiting Fellowship at Wadham College, that allowed me to continue my work in British medieval literature and manuscripts, primarily in Chaucer and Middle English lyrics, with a focus on such theological and especially religious issues as these texts present. The award was named after a former Physics fellow, the legendary Thomas Keeley, who had created the fellowship in his will. I had been a student at Oxford many years earlier, in the 1960's, when I came to know well the late Douglas Gray, then a fellow at Pembroke, subsequently the first J.R.R. Tolkien Professor of Middle English Literature and Language. It was he who had suggested that I apply for the Wadham fellowship, during the course of which Wadham's Chaplain, the Rev. Dr. Giles Fraser, and I set up a program connected to the school in Tower Hamlets where I had taught previously, in which Wadham students would both visit the school once or twice a term, and twice yearly welcome a small group of children from the school to Wadham, who would come, with two or so attending teachers, to spend a day in Oxford. The intention from the beginning was twofold: first of all, to incorporate into the schema of the Bangladeshi children, who the school primarily taught, a sense of what a university was, and to encourage them to understand what its possibilities might be, before the reefs and shoals of early adolescence swept such considerations aside. But it was also intended to offer those undergraduates who wanted it, offering them an opportunity both to try their arm at meeting, interacting with, and teaching racial minority children, and thus to encounter a part of their nation often unknown to them.

We were fortunate in beginning the program at a time when issues of equity were much in the news, thanks partly to then Chancellor of the Exchequer and subsequently Prime Minister, Gordon Brown, who in May of 2000 trumpeted, perhaps unfairly, the case of a would-be British medical student named Laura Spence, who had been refused admission by Oxford but accepted by Harvard. He insisted, and his battle cry was taken up by others, that her case was emblematic of Oxford elitism. But however relevant and possibly useful that intervention may have appeared at the time, the interest and commitment of Giles and subsequently of the Rev. Dr. Harriet Harris, who followed him as Chaplain, mattered far more in launching and sustaining the program. Even so, the larger political circumstance, together with the fact that Wadham was then seen as one of the more progressive Oxford colleges, allowed the program to prosper, gradually and over the years, and if there were fellows who were concerned that it might distract their students from their studies, they very kindly held their fire, perhaps with an eye upon Chancellor Brown's representations, which seemed to go on for the longest time.

It was thus that, for several years after my fellowship came to an end, I would return annually during what is called "second week," in October, when I would offer two lectures on medieval English lyrics in collaboration with Bernard O'Donoghue, Wadham's fellow in medieval English literature, and one of the best living English poets known to me. Also, at the invitation of Wadham's welcoming new Chaplain (now Chaplain of the University of Edinburgh), I would describe the program that Giles and I had begun the year before, during the period of my fellowship, and encourage students to try their arm, as the British say. Harriet soon embraced the program, and proved to be a perceptive and highly effective director, leading it with both sensitivity and evident success for nine of the fifteen years it was in operation, and working through sometimes complicated issues that came up with whomever the Head Teacher was in the Tower Hamlets school. What emerged was a program in which a small number of Wadham undergraduates continued to go once or twice each term to "Anchorage School" in Tower Hamlets to work in the Language Arts, and to speak English with the children, who in turn would visit Wadham twice a year, when they would meet with the students they had already encountered in their school, and thus to begin an acquaintance with higher education. On these visits, the children would have lunch with their student tutors and, after their long ride to Oxford, would run about in Wadham's extensive gardens. Then they would either visit a museum or take part in a "seminar" in Wadham with their tutors, one that involved their work back at Anchorage. The underlying purpose of such visits was to put an understanding of what a university was clearly and happily in the minds of the children, who usually came from years 5 and 6. Another goal was to engage such student tutors as were interested (thanks to Harriett, there was no shortage of student interest) in encountering Tower Hamlets children, who were well outside the tutors' usual range of acquaintances. Whether because of their age, their energy or their interest, university students, whether from Oxford or from Georgetown, make very effective tutors, and it is not un reasonable that, along with everything else they have to think about, they thus begin to consider what their own contribution may be to the world in which they are going to live.

But it would be mistaken to think that what is now called "Outreach" began with the programs I have been describing, which unusually were directed at younger children, since for older students seeking admission there are numerous, often excellent, arrangements already in place to attract and inform them in the year in which they apply. In comparatively recent years individual colleges have taken care that their "Open Days" (two days, usually in July, when the colleges are open to students who might want to apply) acknowledge an interest in ethnic minority students in a way that not all of them had done before. Recently the colleges have placed large banners with the name of the college over their entrances to help student visitors know which college is which. Some colleges have added images of happy students to these banners, and New College's 2019 banner showed a young white male student, a woman student, and a minority student too. St Peter's banner, braver still, showed only a single student who seemed to come from an ethnic minority. These adjustments did not seem to me trivial, and I was reminded of an encounter I had some years ago with the Head Teacher of a large London middle school who was much invested in his minority students, with whom a better-informed colleague and I had been discussing how best to address college entrance. To speed our conversation, and at my colleague's request, I had brought along a large informational pamphlet that I had obtained from the Oxford admissions office, which showed many a happy student on its cover, every one of them white. The Head took up that circumstance at once, with an evident irritation that struck me at the time. Images like that one may not always register if you are white, but they certainly can otherwise. So viva New College, sometimes thought to be a rather grand sort of place, but viva St Peter's too.

These and other practices are now generally encouraged by those offices in the university concerned with Outreach, not simply to satisfy an inquisitive Parliament, but also to expand the university's intellectual and social outreach in its own interests. In recent years too, officials within the university have endorsed certain programs and projects begun in individual colleges as a way both of encouraging them and of making them better known. Thus, it was reported in 2019 that the Oxford college known as Lady Margaret Hall expanded its definition of "under-represented students" to include applicants who have experienced "disadvantage," a general term in Britain, but one that includes those who have been in a position of care. There is a similar program reported at University College, that also takes into account socio-economic considerations, apparently without reference to race. Both of these programs, and others too, require that some academic time be spent in Oxford before any formal program of study begins: a "Foundation Year" at Lady Margaret Hall, and what seems to be quite a short summer program at University College, both of which seek to acclimatize those who would become first year students to the circumstances and the realities of college life.

Such programs are by now effectively stock-in-trade in many American universities, including Georgetown, where they can extend over much of the summer before the academic year begins, and then reach into the new academic year itself. In the four-year course-driven American system, it is possible in some universities for designated students in their first year to elect certain courses that will be part of their formal curriculum and will thus count as requirements toward their degree. In Oxford, summer courses intended to introduce college requirements have expanded greatly, and in 2019 were said to be doubling in size in the more important such programs, so as to include 1,375 high school students. It is possible to discuss such things now because in recent years, the university has become more and more transparent about its admissions. For example, Oxford reported that in 2018 more than 60% of its student body came from state schools, what in America would be called public schools, not from private ones, known paradoxically as "Public Schools" in Britain. In 2019 the university hoped to have as much as 25% of its student body made up of students from disadvantaged backgrounds by 2023, though I doubt the pandemic will have helped it do so.

I understand that there will be those who will believe that I have been treading upon sacred ground, and I admit that my insight into these complex matters is far from perfect. But speaking as a sympathetic outsider, and writing in the happy, pre-pandemic year of 2019, it seemed to me possible that such issues were at last being addressed seriously, particularly on the college level, and that a good beginning was underway.

A Return to Washington

Yet in the end, and in spite of my obvious if practical interest in the admission to higher education of ethnic minority students, my main concern in this book is not with college entrance, but with younger ethnic minority students, and with the ways in which they can be helped both to learn and to teach. In this context, such influence as there was between the American and the British programs I was concerned with went both ways, and some of the practices we developed in Washington were unmistakably informed by what I had seen and learned in Oxford, Cambridge and London. Thus, for example, as the Sursum Corda program advanced in age, it became less, rather than more complicated in its operation. As I have already said, I became disinclined to incorporate testing and evaluation of the learners – formal measurement, if you prefer, and much encouraged by givers of grants – for a variety of reasons. Our learners were, if anything, over-tested in their schools, and they had come to believe that such measurements constituted a demeaning, not a supportive, practice, really intended for others — tests work best for white kids, one learner told me. Besides, as I have been saying, our tutors were unaccustomed to taking measurements, which really are useful only if connected to instruction, as ours never were. There was a brief period when we experimented with Informal Reading Inventories (IRIs), designed to identify individual needs and strengths, and I remember someone associated with one of the other groups at Georgetown expressing surprised admiration, I believe without irony, that we were undertaking the measurement ourselves. He was having them done "professionally," though as I recall, his group, like ours, had no particular application in mind. But we do so love to quantify everything in America, disadvantaged persons too, even as we acknowledge how imprecise and yet how harmful, such measurements sometimes can be.

But the programs with which I became associated in Oxford and then in Cambridge had no time for such hocus-pocus. They differed from the Washington program in that they were directed at older learners among whom the ability to read and write could be assumed, so that their focus was upon content as prescribed by the school curriculum, topics on which tutors and learners could readily communicate. Thus, even if they met infrequently, at least they met over common ground. Because the Washington program was directed at skills and comprehension both – the language arts, which we understood traditionally as reading, writing, speaking and listening – though communication between tutor and learner, particularly at the beginning, could be somewhat difficult.

In such interchanges, one-on-one communication never constituted a promised land, but they were still a way forward, and rested upon a mutual understanding of both short-term objectives, in Washington that the learner should learn to read effectively, or that, in London, he or she should deepen his or her understanding of, for example, the Normans. But there were others as well that were both mutual and long-term -- that the learners should meet those whom they otherwise wouldn't, and one day, like them, attend university. I do not wish to belabor the parallels between the programs. They turned upon like understandings of the role of tutor and learner, but with a greater emphasis on subject matter in London, and on the nature and purpose of a relationship that often addressed skills in Washington, in each case involving an exchange of indeterminate depth. But the regard in which Cambridge students were held by the children in years 5 and 6 when they first visited a London school now some time ago, seemed to me to echo a like situation in Washington long since, in which the children from a family that enrolled in our program worked far more easily with white people as they grew older than other members of the same family who did not. This circumstance may not be paralleled in London, but as a general rule, programs like the ones I have been describing exist far less to judge and measure than to encourage and promote, and to do so without engaging quantity.

The Non-Pedagogical Aspect of Tutoring

Throughout this account I have been suggesting that although the expressed intention of our programs at both Sursum Corda and now at Golden Rule were and are to address the language arts, it quickly became evident that the instruction ran both ways, was not confined to pedagogy, and that our tutors learned, or at least came to understand, as much as they taught. In my experience, students who engage in such programs are invariably sympathetic to and interested in the children whom they seek to serve, though if they do not share their race or their cultural identity they can easily if mistakenly assume that there are few if any real differences to which they need attend.

Whatever else we may be, we are also, at least in part, a precis of our past, though depending upon circumstances, we all can wish for a fuller understanding of the challenges that race and class present. And with that hope can come the other objective of our Washington program, and one we sought for in London too: a means of encouraging our learners to understand what a college or university was, and also that their tutors both enjoyed being there and wanted it for them too, so that it was in every way appropriate they should, in time, seek to attend it. Because the London learners were generally older than the Washington ones, the theme sounded there more easily, and unlike Washington, rarely for the first time. But we sounded it in Washington and with emphasis – though changes having been made, it might resonate in London too.

Thus one of my own hopes for the Georgetown program at Sursum Corda was that at least some of our tutors, young as they were, would not forget their encounter with an even younger person whom they had grown to know and like, and whom otherwise they probably would never have encountered, and that experience would speak to their understanding of others who were unlike themselves. This aspiration was not entirely a fantasy. Some years ago, as I have reported elsewhere, I met a former tutor in Richmond, Kentucky, who remembered in detail, and asked warmly after, the young girl she had once taught at Sursum Corda. Alas, in that case, as in others, I simply did not know. But in Washington, these associations can not only run deep, and sometimes both ways. Young as our tutors and learners both are, the nature of their association is far more than a detail, especially given the insidious and yet somehow open way in which racism operates in America.

One other parallel that struck me much of the time was the way in which minority students, as they became involved in our programs, both in Georgetown and in Oxford, proved to be particularly able in responding to the learners with whom they were working, and quickly committed to their work. At the very end of the Wadham program, when the Chaplain was about to change and the future had become very much in doubt, I encountered a young man who came, from what he told me, from what sounded to have been a disadvantaged background. He was keenly interested in the program as a way of reaching out to those who were like himself, and encouraging them to follow him to Oxford. Such reactions were common, but not universal, in the Georgetown program too, where such minority students as worked with us, fewer than I would have wished, invariably moved most easily among our learners, sometimes even surprising themselves by their evident effectiveness.

But the larger issue, present in each case, was our engagement with younger, rather than older children. In Washington, this meant that issues of race, though present, did not form a barrier between tutor and learner, and their engagement was generally easy and usually happy. By aiming at younger children, our program sought to engage with a recognizable community of almost twenty years standing in which almost no one ever went to college, not everyone finished high school, and illiteracy was not at all unknown. Under such circumstances, literacy was a first concern, but just behind it came our second goal, that college was a possibility for everyone. The parents of our young learners generally supported what we sought to do but were more knowing and open-eyed than we were about the possibilities that we held out. Many of them saw us, however, as a useful alternative to the drug trade, even though certain of them may have been loosely involved with it themselves, usually indirectly, and through a relative. Meanwhile, our students tended to consider their work in generally social terms, though it also touched upon their personal value systems. It would be too easy to say that, even among those who had little or no interest in things religious, their efforts were entirely secular.

The values they drew upon, and by example taught, were certainly rooted in what had been taught to them, but there was choice and selectivity involved as well, present in such a way as to indicate that the personal, humane, and attentive practices that engaged them went beyond a concern for a just society to a deeper sense of how life among mortals should be lived. Particularly if their work continued, it was not difficult to discern a certain complexity to their commitment, a dimension that usually passed unacknowledged among us, but was no less real for that.

How the Sursum Corda Program Worked for its Youngest Learners and Taught its Tutors

I have already briefly described some of the changes the Washington program at Sursum Corda underwent during the last twenty-seven years of its operation. I believe that the most important were these: we saw to it that the tutors went not once, but twice a week to their learners, I among them, always to the same learner (or occasionally to two learners, but in most cases not for long), and that they were not only instructed, but continuously if discreetly overseen in what they taught. Such a relationship between tutor and learner was important throughout our work, which largely took place soon after school, in the early evening, after the learners had returned home and usually had had dinner, so that, refreshed or not, there was a general sense that things could begin again. Over the years we both employed and abandoned other practices, such as primary tests for evaluating performance, and, largely to testify to what we believed were our best practices, we came to adopt three "mottos" that served both to guide our thinking and to offer some kind of direction to beginning tutors.

The first of these, Don't Prompt Too Quickly, was indeed directed at new tutors, and was meant to encourage them not to fear silence when a difficult word presented itself to a learner, and not to rush in with the required word too quickly, as often happened. Simple as it sounds, it really proved an important and difficult direction since, as one tutor told me, "We come to help them read, and if there's a word they don't know we should say it." Not so, I found myself all too often insisting. Patience was what was wanted first of all, and by tutor and learner alike! In due course we made out a list of "Word Attack Strategies," which indeed included "giving" the word, that is, telling the learner what it was, but that practice came last of all. Before it came silence on the tutor's part, repeating the words that came before, and jumping over the word and continuing on, so as to establish overall context and to "get" the word upon returning, among other practices.

The second motto, Comprehension, Comprehension, Comprehension, was a child of whole language, which, changes having been made, certainly informed our program, though for younger children, phonics, through the "phonics first" booklets we used for years, had a role as well. But more than that, a certain focus on comprehension was intended to emphasize to the new tutor that their learner really needed to understand the meaning of the words that they were reading together, and not simply saying what was printed on the page. Their concern was with their learner's capacity for higher thinking, with their metacognitive faculties, not with calling words. With beginning readers, we focused on Previewing, looking over a book or part of one before beginning to read it, so that both tutor and learner could know what to expect. Certain words, like proper nouns and place names, could thus be dealt with in advance, not languished over when they appeared. During the process of reading, particularly if the tutor was reading to the learner (a process we encouraged with high interest texts, particularly those beyond the learner's current range), we also practiced Prediction, in which the tutor would pause at a meaningful or suspenseful moment in the narrative, and ask, "What do you think is going to happen next?" Sometimes the learner would answer, "I don't know, read it and see," but when that happened, the tutor, who at least in theory had examined the passage the night before, was to insist gently for an answer, even resorting to writing down what the learner then replied, a strategy that almost always guaranteed an answer of some sort, and kept learner and tutor both well focused upon the meaning of what was being said.

As we moved away from beginning readers, these practices remained when needed, but what we called FIAT questions became the bread and butter of our program.

I am going to pause on these questions, in order to give a sense of how our program proceeded, since these questions were instrumental in teaching our learners to learn, and our tutors to teach. Although there were other strategies on which we depended, these were at our core, and aided both in encouraging the comprehension we sought, and also, by the exchange they initiated, in helping our tutors to develop a relationship with the learners they served. For many years, most of our learners came instructed to some degree in phonics, a strategy widely employed in D.C. schools, but many were less familiar with comprehension, in understanding what it was that they had just read, or had just been read to them. As time went by we came to employ four quite traditional kinds of questions, not asked in any particular order, and often focusing on only one or two in any given tutorial. They are called FIAT questions, and I name them here: Factual questions, Interpretive questions, Applicative questions, and Transactive questions. In a certain way they could work together, but in fact each had its own office, and their intended effect was to encourage our learners to understand the texts that we placed before them, and so to read with Comprehension, Comprehension, Comprehension, a state of mind that learners and tutors alike could understand, embrace and communicate. I shall return to them in greater depth in the next chapter, when I describe which of our former practices we brought, albeit changed, into the program we organized during the pandemic, and here only note their effect in encouraging communication between learner and tutor alike.

What all these questions (less often the Factual, but even that one, depending upon circumstances) have in common is that they serve to develop a deeper interest in the meaning of a text than a learner might otherwise be inclined to take, particularly if encouraged to do so. They can address and deepen understanding, usually of particular moments in a narrative, and in doing so speak, if indirectly, to issues of overall comprehension. Except for such personal exchanges as took place, the best, most meaningful conversations between learners and tutors in our program were almost always the result of FIAT questions. Thus, for the longest time (by which I mean our first two decades), these two mottos, Don't Prompt Too Quickly, and Comprehension, Comprehension, Comprehension, were what we embraced and repeated, and assisted by Previewing and Prediction strategies and by FIAT questions, they became the strategies that guided our work.

There is one final aspect to our work in Washington that took place only at Golden Rule, not at Sursum Corda, and that does not fit in easily elsewhere, so I shall describe it here. In 2020, not long before the pandemic made itself known, we introduced a practice of having many of the tutors begin their tutorials by exchanging a greeting and a few words with their learner in a non-English language that the tutor knew well. The inspiration came from a particularly perceptive and smart tutor named Orlando, who had employed his fluent Italian, acquired in youth by tutorial when his family was living in Italy, to engage his learner in their tutorial, thought in practice they did no more than to greet each other, and agree to begin work. Their practice had begun during our third year at Golden Rule when they were reading an English translation of that wonderful French children's book, *Asterix et Obelix*, replete with many a pun, and the narrative had taken its protagonists to Italy. Michael, Orlando's learner, had become intrigued with Italy, whether because of the book or, more likely, because of his tutor. In any case, he was soon beginning each tutorial by saying, "Ciao! Mi ciamo Michele!" To this Orlando would reply, "Ciao, Michele! Mi ciamo Orlando! Andiamo a studiare." Their conversation then moved on to English, but the initial exchange seemed to help Michael, a somewhat reserved boy, step out of himself and engage with their work, reading and writing in English, more easily.

We put our plan into practice on March 3, 2020, calling a short meeting of tutors and learners together in the room where we give our tutorials before we began work, so that everyone would know what we were about to do. There was immediate and genuine interest from our learners, and to everyone's delight, it went almost exactly as planned. At the session's end three of our learners rushed up to me, their tutors close behind, to demonstrate their newfound skill. Two others did so as we were walking out.

We discussed this practice in seminar, and agreed that it held out promise for everyone, not only because the learners took to it with a will, but also because it seemed to us to offer encouragement for time to come, whether to study another language, or to reach beyond what, too often, was expected of them. But we also agreed that the practice was not to be required, that the learner could end it if he or she wanted to (none did), and that the tutor would put it into practice only if he or she felt confident enough to do so. The languages we employed were several, Spanish most of all, but also Italian, French and Chinese, and again, only a handful of words were expected from everyone. We had just put it into practice when the pandemic struck and we all went home, and the online circumstances of our tutoring when the schools were closed and we continued to tutor online – discussed in chapters 6 to 8 following – were not conducive to maintaining it in operation, so after only two or three meetings it came to an end, at least for now.

And this: about this time too we had just begun to experiment with playing a few bars -- or a little more -- of classical music after the tutors arrived, but before we began work, and then again a few more at the end of the session, to signal that it was ending. The intention was both to settle the mood and also to introduce a few strains of such music into the lives of tutors and learners alike. We began with one of the Brandenburg Concertos -- the fifth, I believe -- and ended with some bars from "The Magic Flute," though I cannot recall now which ones. One of the tutors had reasonably argued for Vivaldi instead of Mozart, but in the end we used what we had at hand.

Alas, our technology failed us, ironic in view of what was to come. But our speakers were not strong enough to fill either of the the two rooms in which we worked, and unlike our venture into language learning, our musical ducks were not in a row when COVID brought us down. But our too-soft speakers made me wonder if it might be possible to play such music sottovoce during tutorials in the future, when we get them up and running again. We'll see. It was still in the experimental phase.

Politics and Patrons

Throughout the more than thirty years that these programs have been in operation, we fought shy of identifying them with any political party, movement, or current cause. The reasons for this were numerous and no doubt obvious, but among them was the circumstance that our tutors were at a point in their lives when they were developing values, attitudes, and assumptions of their own, ones that were as yet somewhat inchoate, and we did not want to require of them more than that to which they had already put their hand. In general, their inclinations tended to be slightly leftward, but not precipitously so, and what we sought instead of politics pure and simple was to cross racial and cultural lines that many had hardly encountered before, at least consciously, and to experience them thoughtfully.

Thus, our discussions in class were largely pedagogical, and concerned the strategies we employed, FIAT questions among them, and the effect these were having on our learners. As we encountered the changed circumstances of Golden Rule Apartments, however, certain of James Baldwin's essays, and Toni Morrison's extraordinary novel *Beloved* entered the lists, and occasionally current topics would also present themselves for discussion.

But at the beginning of September, 2014, the killing by the police of Mr. Michael Brown the preceding August in Fergusson, Missouri, deeply engaged a class that was just beginning to encounter some of the realities that obtained at Sursum Corda. Both then and the following April, when the equally shocking killing of Mr. Freddie Gray took place in Baltimore, our usual pedagogical discretion took a new turn. I believe it was the Baltimore killing, being close at hand, that served most to engage us, so that we added a third motto to the two I have already named, one we owed quite consciously to Mohandas Gandhi: "Be the Change that You want to See." I am told that what Gandhi actually said was, "You must be the change that…," but given our youthful and voluntary circumstances, we dispensed with the first two words. Still, the injunction registered with us, perhaps particularly at the time, but subsequently too, even though we knew (at least some of us did) that it was employed rather widely in programs and places other than our own.

In this context, I should mention that Gandhi (1869-1948) figured in our program in another way too, and had done so long before he contributed our third motto. For some time, we had listed four persons whom we deemed what we called our patrons, of whom Gandhi, with whom we shared a love of both peace and non-violence, was one. The other three included St Thomas Aquinas (c. 1225-74), Rev. Dr. Martin Luther King, Jr. (1929-68), and, somewhat to my later chagrin, the once brilliant, if finally unstable, musician Jimi Hendrix (1942-70). The first of these three, Aquinas, we adopted to indicate, if only to ourselves, that we took the pedagogical and academic dimensions of our program seriously, and we did so when oversight of Georgetown students taking part in such programs was minimal. Dr. King we also much honored, in his case for his willingness to enlist whites in his great cause, and for his profound commitment to justice.

Jimi Hendrix had been proposed by a waggish undergraduate who understood too well that my knowledge of such persons was likely to be far from complete. He represented that it was a necessary balance to our solemnity, and as the adoption was supported by his friends, I acquiesced. There things stood for several years, until the circumstances of Jimi Hendrix's life, which were not entirely above reproach, were made known to me by a good friend who is no stranger to irony, and I began to consider that perhaps Jimi Hendrix should be dethroned. Such an action could not be undertaken unilaterally, I reckoned, particularly as I proposed supplanting him with one of my own heroes, Marie Clay, the brilliant New Zealand educator and author to whom our program really did owe a debt. And she was a woman, I pointed out to the tutors, as none of our other patrons were.

Alas, my proposal was rejected with the riposte that our list was of long-standing (this was before the addition of our third motto), and besides, one clever young man asked whether, as she was still living, I was sure that Marie Clay would really welcome membership in a group whose other members included St. Thomas Aquinas, Rev. Dr. Martin Luther King, Jr., and Mohandas Gandhi? Georgetown students are sometimes capable of such sophistry, and so I did not insist, but let things lie, waiting for a more propitious hour, or so I thought. Foolishly, however, I never took the dethronement up again, and then Sursum Corda came to an end.

Dress Codes and Endings

Members of our program could wax eloquent over such diversions, ones of which many of its tutors, perfectly reasonably, took no heed. There were, as well, practicalities that tutors also might ignore, for reasons good and bad. Rather too often I would have to remind tutors to wear t-shirts (when it was warm) or sweat shirts (as autumn drew in) that identified them, by their printed insignia, with our university, both when we came for tutoring, and, rather more importantly, when the tutors went down on a Saturday to take their young learners to a movie at Union Station (no longer possible with our Golden Rule learners, alas, since the movie theater has closed down). Other trips included expeditions to the National Mall, there to play running games and visit a museum, usually with lunch included, during which eating with utensils was, by me at least, sometimes required. My thinking about tutors and Georgetown sweatshirts on such expeditions was that their wearers could thus be identified by the drug people as Georgetown tutors and so left alone, as usually happened. Otherwise, they were of an age in which coming to Sursum Corda could indicate a less noble enterprise, and they would be offered drugs. In this at least I practiced what I preached, and would wear a Georgetown sweatshirt myself on our bi-weekly visits, in order to testify that, in spite of my antiquity, I was neither a City official of any sort, nor an undercover police officer.

At our Christmas party at Sursum Corda, to which a smattering of parents regularly came, and at our spring picnic, which formerly took place on the esplanade on top of

Georgetown's Leavey Center but subsequently moved to the lawn beside the Georgetown Observatory, we read aloud the learners' contributions to our little Kinko's-produced literary magazine; ate pizza and whatever else the tutors produced, drank fruit juice lavishly, and (in the spring at least) allowed the learners to run about as they pleased. At such times I myself reverted to my place of origin and wore a Boston College sweatshirt instead of my usual Georgetown one -- evidence, I suppose, of the rock from which I was hewn.

I hope I may end this looking backward chapter on such an inelegant note. In some ways, what I remember best about our program's early days was the confidence I had each October that we were finally launched again, and the sense each April that we were coming to an end, though in the fall we would rise again, so there was actually no ending to what we did. Perhaps in one sense what we were doing was inventing education, doing what was needed when it was needed and where, and for the most part doing so with joy. I said in the beginning of this account that what I would offer here was no handbook, no how-to-do-it account, but simply a record of our practices, one in which I make the only partly true claim that what I have written here represents our life together. As our learners learned to read, as we learned who they were and who we were, as we admired, or loved, or were indifferent to one another, we reached out to a future that will one day come about, that will be ours to reckon with, and that we now regard with hope and anticipation, even as we seek, in a very small way, to inform it.

Chapter 6

O Brave New World:
University Outreach
During a Time of Pandemic

August 24, 2020

It has been a summer in which nothing has happened but everything has happened; a time in which our three-year literacy project in Washington, D. C. both came to an end and continued more or less as before; in which our genuine regret for everything we had lost when Georgetown University switched to virtual instruction, mixed uneasily with hope and guarded expectation for the year ahead.

As I have described it, Georgetown University's oldest literacy outreach program, at a community known as Sursum Corda, operated for forty-seven years in a low rise, 199 multi-unit community for forty-seven years, the last twenty-seven of which I have described in chapters one through three. When Sursum Corda was finally seized by developers and leveled our program transferred, in September 2017, to Golden Rule Apartments, a nine-story apartment building which stood a block away, where we were again fortunate in our community associations, working first with Mr. Patrick Williams, then with Mr. William Foster, and now with Mr. Frederick Hawkins, all of whom were working with and for Mission First of Philadelphia, the organization that owns and operates the building. In what follows I will describe what happened after March 2020, and then what followed in September of the same year, when Georgetown, like many other universities, lurched into virtual instruction as the coronavirus took root among us, and expectations everywhere were swept away.

Online courses are nothing new in American universities – though until last semester they were uncommon at Georgetown – but I do not know them to have been employed in outreach courses like the one at Golden Rule Apartments, where face-to-face engagement between young undergraduate teacher and even younger learner is usually taken as a matter of course. But conditions being what they were, Georgetown's classes ended on campus in March 2020, and soon thereafter went online. At that point tutors, learners and professors alike, had little choice but to see if everything could be made to work again, under admittedly disadvantageous conditions. So we all took a breath, and began again with a will.

The interchanges that developed thereafter between Georgetown students and Golden Rule children, or between tutors and learners, as we call ourselves, took place initially over the telephone in that suddenly cut-short semester, and supplied moments of laughter, tranquillity, and momentary relief to tutors and learners both, occasionally rising to the level of instruction in books read or remembered together. Our practice, in those first chaotic days, was for tutors to call and speak to one of our learners' parents or care-givers before going on to their learner him or herself, explaining their new now virtual role, and seeking permission to proceed. When one mother turned her phone over to her two school-aged daughters she had pretended that she didn't know who these "college girls" on the phone could possibly be. But her daughters shrieked their tutors' names, and settled down for an hour-long conversation. Many of the Georgetown students had been as upset as their learners by the turn of events, even as they left their university, and returned, usually with much reluctance, to their homes. "Confused, angry, and upset," was the way one young man, more honest than most, described his reaction to the sudden violent transplant that banished him from Georgetown, at no notice at all, and sent him to live at home instead. But the Golden Rule tutors quickly reached out to their learners, as to young but also old friends.

Yet in spite of everything, the summer following that chaotic March proved time enough for faculty and administrators to decide what, the coronavirus notwithstanding, might be allowed to continue when classes resumed again in the fall. By May, my own considerations had been aided by a number of colleagues who shared my sense that we should continue to offer, if only virtually, as many outreach courses as possible, including the undergraduate literacy outreach course I have been describing, formerly at Sursum Corda, but now at Golden Rule Apartments, almost five miles from the campus, in which a small class of ten students was already enrolled for the fall semester. In the normal course of things, I would have increased it to fifteen, but there was nothing normal about 2020. It soon became apparent that another course I offered, one that required students to work as teachers' aides in two urban schools, would have to be cancelled, since the students were all now at home, miles from the classrooms in which they would have had to labor. Still, in the Golden Rule program, tutor and learner worked one-on-one, and that circumstance allowed for the possibility that we could continue the course, if only online.

And things went on from there. By July I had grasped that if a tutorial program between Georgetown undergraduates and children at Golden Rule Apartments was to continue, it would be most useful to have some support from the department and perhaps the university as well, and not all of it virtual. Dr. Ricardo Ortiz, who had from the first had supported the program's move from Sursum Corda to Golden Rule, was encouragement itself, and our able Director of Undergraduate Studies, Dr. Daniel Shore, was equally helpful. Fortunately too, a former Golden Rule tutor, recently graduated, named Bradley Galvin, was available to help with the course, and thankfully he proved willing to become involved again at Golden Rule. Bradley's American Studies senior thesis, video but not virtual, had examined the last days of Sursum Corda, and showed a critical and informed engagement with that place. His assistance to me had been encouraged and materially assisted by Dr. Randy Bass, an old friend who had become not only a Professor of English but also the Vice President for Strategic Education Initiatives, and who both shared our interest in such work and also understood it; best of all he considered that it might become useful to others. This mattered because Bradley and I had separately concluded that words like "useful" were not ones invariably attached to our program even by sympathetic observers, particularly when doing so involved the disbursement of money. True enough, we sought to cross boundaries of race, culture, social and economic status and sometimes, when we couldn't get the balance right, gender, but the opposing argument seemed to be that the participants were too young to understand what we were about, at least for now. Let me not reprise the counterargument here, which may suggest itself to anyone who reads these pages sympathetically, but simply echo *New York Times* columnist David Brooks, and suggest that one of the less attractive aspects of America today is the extent to which we all live in isolation from each other, an isolation quite unconnected to the pandemic. But such boundaries were what our program crosses nightly, and with participants who are of an age when beginning again is quite possible.

Beginning Again

Thanks to the coronavirus, the circumstances we faced certainly seemed to us the worst of times, but even so, as we planned and prepared to rise again on only virtual wings, we took comfort in the suggestion that that what we hoped to do had not actually been tried before, or at least not in the way we hoped to do it. But what Randy, Bradley, and I also agreed upon was that our venture, however promising, was thus far a tale without an ending. If we could make these connections real, both among the returning tutors and their learners, and also among those among both groups whom we had yet to meet, a resolution might, in time, present itself. And it was with that thought that, in early August, we spoke on the phone together, cementing our alliance, and Randy, in his office as Associate Provost, generously agreed to supply any financial support we might need, though upon reflection I am inclined to believe that he probably meant within reason. Still, earlier in the summer I had circulated some "Working Notes" among friends and colleagues whom I believed interested in our undertaking, saying what I thought we were likely to confront if we renewed our program in the fall, and almost everyone responded with encouragement and welcome offers of help. So, whatever happened, it seemed that we would have some allies with whom to share our difficulties, when they came calling.

Past Practices

Those Working Notes, which I here summarize, had focused primarily on what I thought we might preserve from our past practices, and also on what probably needed to change. Two principles that underlay our three-year project at Golden Rule Apartments had been carried over unchanged from the previous twenty-seven-year program at nearby Sursum Corda, a community that, as I have already written, had fallen prey to drugs and to development (more to the latter than the former), but which in any case was now no more. These principles insisted that a one-on-one relationship between tutor and learner was essential for progress (though necessarily overseen in the interests of both), and that the tutor should be well instructed in his or her craft, that is, the tutor must know what the program's pedagogical goals were, and how to achieve them. In practice, that meant both seeing to it that tutor/learner relationships, though sometimes close, were never private, and being certain that our tutors were well instructed in how to proceed in their tutorials. The stock-in-trade of a Georgetown tutor is that he or she well understands the reason for, and the practice of, previewing and predicting strategies, and also the use and purpose of FIAT questions: Factual Questions (the simplest of the four, questions that can be answered from only one citation in the text); Interpretive Questions (which usually require two or more citations, and often involve the question "Why?"); Applicative Questions (which place the learner within the text itself, and sometimes evoke unconnected responses: "I'd get my father's gun," one Sursum Corda boy replied, when asked how he would deal with a suddenly appearing lion); and Transactive Questions, (which involve matters of personal value). It is with this strategy and these questions that, before a shared text, many a Georgetown student has learned to ply his or her craft. The tutor of course understands that the goal of the exercise is not to identify, still less simply to sound out, individual words, but to achieve a comprehension of what is being read, and to do so in such a way as to result in meaningful conversation. FIAT questions are not ends in themselves, but they are the way forward into more abstract reasoning, and into the greater maturity that brings.

Thus FIAT questions have proved almost unqualifiedly useful in our work. Changes having been made, the practices they called for became our givens, and we estimated that probably they should be retained in any new world order, like the one that now confronted us. They were certainly compatible with the online electronic program we had tried to adapt, not entirely successfully, when we turned to virtual instruction in March. It is called the Raz-Kids program, and which was first pointed out to us by Patrick Williams, when he was Resident

Manager at Golden Rule. And the more I saw of the program the more I liked it. Its great advantage is that it allows the tutor to select a book at the right level for the learner, and then to read that book simultaneously, sharing it on a screen (the tutor's), and so to read the same text together, with the tutor asking comprehension questions based on the reading, either employing ones that are provided, or (better) following our practice of employing comprehension questions that could lead the learner not only to show an understanding of what is being read, but also to the virtual purchase, from points earned, of virtual prizes, a practice that seems calculated to encourage tutor and learner to get to know each other in the process. What I also liked about the program, to tell the truth, was how compatible it appears to be with our present practices, to such strategies as previewing and predicting, and how easily it lends itself to FIAT questions. But from the beginning (or at least from March 2020), it was clear that change was in the cards if we were actually to carry our program into the next academic year, and the first Raz-Kids program seemed to me the most promising way forward.

By the time the new academic year began again, everything was beginning to make sense. The common denominator of our program both at Sursum Corda, where our learners included many K-3 children, and also at Golden Rule Apartments, where the children tended to be somewhat older, had been that all participants met all together, twice a week and for an hour each time, and though their ways of then proceeding differed according to cases, their ends were all but identical. We guessed, of course, that there would be changes in the fall. What we expected was more flexibility, which I hoped would not mean less coherence. But once they had checked in with the parent or care-giver in charge, and obtained permission to enter this new domain, our tutors would enter virtually into their learner's apartment twice weekly, and after the first time, they would come in effectively uninvited. How often they might do so, and for how long, would need to be negotiated. This process might prove easier for the tutors who had already worked in the program than for our novices, who would not have a point of reference yet, and might not only feel a little green, but be so. Time would tell, but I could see that I would have to urge both flexibility and commitment on both parties, and from the very first. It may not be easy. As they say in Brittany, the sea is great; our boat is very small.

But before we sally forth again, I should not fail to thank those at Golden Rule Apartments, and those at its parent organization, Mission First, for having been so helpful while these new arrangements were being made. I have already mentioned Mr. Patrick Williams, who was so very helpful throughout, but who, in July this year, moved to another position. But through the good advice of my friend Shiv Newaldass, who made some very useful calls on our behalf, Officer Darrin Bates, who quite literally showed us the way there, and through the equally good offices of Elizabeth Everhart, Pamela Graves, and others, we came in the end to Mr. William Foster at Golden Rule, with whom we have now connected, and who is likely to be our main connection there. I am, of course, much pleased, and somewhat relieved, that this is so. Our programs at Sursum Corda and Golden Rule Apartments, like many another, took their life not only from pedagogical knowledge and the kind of unequal but real friendships that can exist between older and younger young people, but also from the surrounding community in which they live and work, and through the web of such organizations as support them. It was gratifying, over the course of the summer, to hear expressions of support and confidence from many to whom I spoke, and to learn that our work over the past three years had been both known and understood, and so had earned good wishes for the coming year.

We Begin Again at Golden Rule Apartments:
September 3, 2020

But while academic challenges abound, I believe I have found, in something called the Raz-Kids Program (it can be googled), a way to connect tutors and learners via Zoom, while putting the same books into the hands of both at the same time. At first I wondered how we might bring the program into what we do, but thanks to Randy and Bradley, I think we have found a way. As I write this I have now had, on August 26th, my first online meeting with the tutors, which was both a joy and a challenge. They are indeed scattered around the country with a concentration here in Georgetown, and several of those who enrolled were in the program last March, and some who were not are friends with those who were, so our gathering on Zoom, though informed, also feels a little *gemütlich*, that word for which there is no English equivalent, but suggests a friendly sense that what we feel and think together matters most of all. I had guessed, and even been a little concerned, that such might be the case, and had changed the syllabus accordingly, with inclusions so obvious as not to need defending. A few works by and about Black American authors come first of all, and I will ask a reckoning of what they make of them in their course papers, when they discuss what they think they have taught, and also what they have learned during the semester.

But after one class the tutors have taught me that they are indeed a match for this brave new world we're living in, and that's for sure. They may be physically distant from their learners, but if we can recapture those moments of informal education that we do best of all, we can probably learn among ourselves what's working best, or could be. I have not required these essays and narratives before, when students learned directly from those they taught, and needed instruction only how to teach them in return. They also learned from one another, and then they learned to speak in their own voices. Teaching and learning come not from printed texts, but from what is here and now, and what we see together, even in print.

The upshot is that things will be different now – even as we make them as they were. The learners are at arm's length, certainly. I peer at my students, and they at theirs, on a glowing screen. Some tutors bridge that gap too easily (I hope I do), but need reminding that one gap is race. So, we'll read Toni Morrison's *Beloved*, America's new, brilliant, *Moby Dick*, and work out how its fierce white whale, cold slavery, has become the kind of racism we can live with, and that it's far from dead. But before that James Baldwin, whom I first taught decades ago, at Lehigh. I can still remember defending him to a Black student who didn't like him very much at all: "He writes like Whitey," the young man said. "Would that we could," I answered, which amused him. We'll begin with "Equal in Paris," my favorite. They can read it online, gratis, and be reminded that racism cannot be cured with an apology and a check, so that in America as elsewhere, we are going to have one hell of a time getting it out the door.

September 10

But before James Baldwin, FIAT questions again. These are at the center of what we do, even with the welcome assistance of Raz-Kids, without which I doubt our tutoring would prosper as it has. But the interchange between tutor and learner involves questions that lead the learner into understanding the text he or she has just read, and cement the bond that ties them both together. Thus, even though both tutor and teacher employ what I have already called FIAT questions, the actual use of these questions differs markedly. In the classroom, such questions can easily lead to a directed and correct understanding of the meaning of the text, one shared by all (or almost all) the students in the class. One strategy for such an accomplishment is directed reading, or as a Directed-Reading-Thinking-Activity (DRTA), as it is still sometimes called. But the use of DRTA in tutorials of the kind I have been discussing can be problematic. Apart from simple questions of fact, from which there is no escape, there are usually unspoken, sometimes important, questions, implicit in the interchange between tutor and learner, more personal than can appear in class, especially for the learner.

I do not mean to make too much of this, which is rarely a problem in practice, given a smart tutor. But it offers a reason for using FIAT questions in tutorials, or whenever working one-on-one, an understanding that 'works' differently than in that in a classroom setting. A like example appears in repeated reading, which can be a hard sell, but which, echoing one of my teachers, I have come to believe an especially helpful strategy, particularly with beginning readers. It was our stock-in-trade at Sursum Corda, especially in the old days, but is less so now at Golden Rule, where the learners are often older. My experience has been that tutors sometimes need to be encouraged to use it, and will occasionally fight shy of returning to a field already ploughed (as one tutor put it, years ago), and not to understand its usefulness for reading comprehension and fluency. Still, in both of these cases, as in others, the tutor is not only working in support of the classroom teacher. He or she is also, indeed primarily, acting in the interests of the learner, with everything that implies, albeit with some difficulty. FIAT questions at once set free but also direct the tutor's efforts, and lead, so it is hoped, to mutual understanding.

A Digression

To turn from things strictly academic for a moment, I would probably be failing somewhat in my responsibilities if I failed to mention that, founded in 1789 (or thereabouts: the first student did not arrive until years later), Georgetown is the oldest Catholic institution of higher education in the United States, and partly as a result of that attachment, Catholic Social teaching, or as it might be better called in our case, Catholic Social Tradition, figures in the work we undertake. In many ways, it would be impossible to designate as specifically Catholic what we seek to accomplish, since such moral imperatives as we embrace were not limited either to Catholicism or indeed to Christianity, and, broadly stated, are to be found in many traditions. Nor over the years did I do so, insisting instead that our work in course was by no means limited to Catholic students, or to students who thought themselves religious. This should have surprised no one, since the sentiments and beliefs that move us are present in many religions, in Islam and in Judaism, in Hinduism and in almost all Protestant denominations with the possible exceptions of such evangelical groups as privileged the worship of the divine apart from all things else. The forms of expression are numerous, but in the Catholic tradition I would cite a passage in Pope Benedict XVI's 2005 encyclical *Deus Caritas Est*, "God Is Love," no. 30 b, wherein the Pope expresses "gratitude and appreciation to all who take part" in such activities, perceptively adding that "For young people, this widespread involvement constitutes a school of life which offers them a formation in solidarity and in readiness to offer others not simply material aid but their very selves."

Our program thus maintained a kind of double focus, engaging both learners and learning, and our belief remained that concern for others was not an optional extra to literacy tutoring, but a present if not often visited component of what we thought and did. In fact, the more obvious distinctions that appeared among tutors were usually by their disciplines, and it has long been my sense that students studying business or economics or medicine or nursing were at least as likely to be attracted to the work we do as many a one in the humanities, who sometimes believed themselves so familiar with what we were about as to be disinclined actually to take part. Thus, although neither our tutors nor I would have insisted upon it, our work, rooted as it is in an effective and often felt concern for someone who is not me, might sometimes be described as having a dimension that might reasonably be designated as religious, one that often seemed to be attached to Catholic Social Teaching, though not of course in every case.

But I should not represent myself as an entirely uncritical admirer of every discussion of Catholic social teaching as has come my way, some of which have seemed to me more invested in theory and theology than in effective practice, and, whenever individual projects are cited, to suggest (sometimes by way of praise offered or withheld) that the actors involved were most accomplished when their work resonated with a devout agenda. Ours by no means did so, though what it could have responded to may have been rather an element of joy. Not at every moment, to be sure, but more often than you might expect, and on many a return trip to the university, after an evening's work, this tutor or that one would exclaim, often with surprise, that his or her work had been invigorating in a way not expected, and evident pleasure was in the voice that spoke. One ironic result was that, each year, I had to enjoin students not to come to tutoring if they were ill or even infectious, and during our years at Sursum Corda there developed a credited tradition that if a student had an important exam the following morning, he or she usually scored appreciably higher if tutoring was attended to the night before. In my experience, religious engagement among the young is happiest in action and outcome, in which such traditions as the ones we followed certainly can play a part, but are no less real for that, even when, or especially when, socially constructed. And I do not imply at all that our joys are denied to the more conventionally religious, whom as a general rule made excellent and conscientious tutors, even as they induced a moment of not entirely welcome self-reflection in me.

These last two paragraphs are of course a digression, not entirely germane to the present semester, in which attachments to learners and to the program, so essential for our work, are already apparent, and with luck will see us through.

Underway: September 21

But to return, if only in summary, to what we have become. After almost two weeks, we have now largely arranged assignments, that is, agreed which tutor will work with which learner. This has not been difficult overall, less so than in more conventional years, since as I have said already, half the class has carried over from last semester and the individual tutors will remain with the learners they have been instructing already. Our beginning tutors appear willing take on whomever they are presented with. Miley, one of our "best" learners (most enthusiastic, thoughtful, eager to learn), has already linked up with Isobel, or Izzy as she is called, a bright, energetic and perceptive young woman from London, who looks to be perfect for the job, since Miley was taught last year by one of our very best tutors, since lost to graduation, who was in no small part contributory to whom she has become. Another new tutor, Jack Berson, is much interested in what we are about because he has his eye on a future project, one led by Bradley that may one day come about. I ask him to tutor the only learner in this cohort who is not associated with Golden Rule Apartments, nor living therein, whose name I had from my former Sursum Corda colleague, Christine Nicholson. And Mr. Foster has already helped us with yet a third learner, whose electronic connections seemed at first to have disappeared. But it was not so, and thanks to him we are back on track. Needless to say, all of this took more time and energy than it takes to tell, but at least as much as FIAT questions, they are central to what we do, and I make no apology for bending your ear. But we still need to be certain that our learners are in fact connected, and if so how, and whether they yet understand Raz-Kids, and how, in fact, out instruction is to flourish.

But this semester has been different in another way as well, different from last, when we were all online. More or less obviously, the students as a whole have become accustomed to our new conventions, "resigned to our fate," as one of them put it. But their resignation is not without its advantages. If anything, they are more attentive, more focused, than they were last semester, whether virtually or face-to-face. The reasons are not hard to find. For one thing the students are, as it were, "at home," whether literally, at home with parents and siblings, or as seemed to me as often, in a shared house. Whichever, it is the time we have together that effectively makes them students, so they remain alert, and this semester at least, attentive to what is being said, perhaps particularly by their colleagues. This is not less true in my Chaucer class, though I shall need to see their first paper to know how deeply it has set in. But practically, I have no complaints at all. Though in a class like Sursum Corda, committed to outreach as it is, I remain alert for any evidence of adjustment, partly to welcome it, partly to see what needs to change.

Reading Aloud

And this: the longer I worked with young children at Sursum Corda (as noted, there are fewer such at Golden Rule), the more I came to believe that the ability of a child not only to read, but to do so fluently and with confidence, was helped, often greatly, when he or she read aloud and to others, words from a printed text, an action which could prove as meaningful as the act of reading itself. The first time a very young learner speaks printed words was the moment (dare I say so?)

when the act of speaking mattered more than that of understanding, when the ability to communicate to another what lies printed between them, matters more than anything at all. With us that "other person" was almost always a tutor (we had more public readings at our end-of-semester parties), whose duty it was to recognize what had been said, to understand its significance, and to respond. And though for a moment that experience of hearing printed words spoken might be limited to one other, it would not continue so, since it is in the nature of things that others will soon be admitted to audience, as life goes on.

Reading aloud has always been important in schools as well, but in tutoring, and with beginning readers, it had a different role, one that was at the heart of what we undertook, and served to validate our program, while freeing our young learners into life. At Sursum Corda often, and very occasionally at Golden Rule, it was or is the primary concern for the one-on-one tutorials we give. As always, our larger focus is on reading comprehension, but with that comes the simple act of reading texts aloud, first showing a way into the greater world that literacy brings, but also offering a way into ourselves, and knowing we can say the truths we hold.

At the end of each semester, at least until the pandemic struck, we would for years conclude each semester with the presentation to parents, care-givers, children and tutors alike of a little, Kinko's-produced "literary magazine," made up of our learners' written work (together with a few words added by their tutors). At a celebratory party, each learner would read aloud what he or she had written, to the rest of us. Refreshments and (at the end of the first semester) modest Christmas presents (usually inscribed books) from the tutors were waiting, but they never intruded upon our ritual, and I was pleased year after year at how willingly our young learners sat undistracted (for the most part) in what amounted to respectful silence to hear their classmates read, clapped after-

wards, and very willingly (usually) took their own turn thereafter. For a child to read aloud, to others, words that he or she
has put together, seemed to me at the heart of what we did, if
not at the heart of civilization too.

How We Live Now: September 25

Bradley calls just as I am about to start an online interview, so
we say only a few words to each other, but I am not uninter-
ested in what concerns him. Later we speak at length, and it
emerges that he has called Randy to report our progress, and
while doing so had said that things have not been moving as
quickly as he had hoped with the Raz-Kids program, which is
very much his chief interest. I am not sure what Randy made
of this, but he reasonably advised Bradley to hold individual
tutorials with the students in order to be sure they all know
how to connect. But as we speak, it emerges that Bradley has
misunderstood the number of students in our class, and so
believed that it is larger than it is, and that there are more students without learners than are. I point this out, and suggest
that really only a few have yet to sign on to Raz-Kids, and
add that I have just sent an email to one and all asking compliance by next Wednesday, though without actually using
the word compliance so as not to discomfort the electronically
challenged. I quote what was the first motto (long since abandoned) of our Sursum Corda program, *Festina lente,* "Make
haste slowly," but add that offering individual tutorials is a
great idea, and of course we will do so. I sympathize with
the young man's impatience, the more so since Bradley has
a greater plan in mind, and hopes in due course to oversee
a like online tutoring program between Georgetown undergraduates and the descendants of the 272 slaves whom the
university unconscionably sold to pay its debts in 1838, now
living in Louisiana, a project which is itself part of an even
larger agenda in which it appears that the university is now

much invested. I had reminded Bradley that I had already sent the class one email concerning Raz-Kids, but now I send a second, announcing the "good news" that Bradley has very kindly offered to give individual tutorials to any among them who would like help connecting their learner to the Raz-Kids program. And not long thereafter one of our tutors emails me to arrange one. So all is well again. Festina lente.

Two days later Bradley calls again, and he has now had a tutorial with his learner, using Raz-Kids, and it could not have gone better. He has reached the seven-year-old boy he is teaching in his Golden Rule Apartment, and wise man that he is, did not plunge right into teaching, but sought to establish a friendly relationship first, based upon football and listening to each other. Best of all, the boy knows Raz-Kids from school, takes to it easily, and is delighted not only to read the book Bradley had chosen, but insists upon taking the quiz at the end, which will win him 150 points (plus 50 for having read the book) with which he can 'buy' a virtual helmet and shirt and a virtual dog named Bingo. Expertly, Bradley has employed FIAT questions throughout his tutorial, all four kinds he reports, and notes that they worked to perfection (or near-perfection) on the texts that he and his learner read together. He also allows that his own virtual background, that shows a large, friendly llama that looks out from just behind his head, and he reckons that that was a help as well, if only as an icebreaker.

When we meet as a class he describes his experience, and it has the desired effect. The two students who have fought shy of using Raz-Kids immediately sign up for a tutorial with Bradley, and promise to put what they learn there into practice. One other tutor has had an experience similar to Bradley's, all the better because he is teaching a slightly older learner for whom the Raz-Kids enticements have not yet proved quite as effective. Two others have employed only the reading function, but not the quiz function, which they now embrace. Bravo Bradley.

The proof of any pudding is of course in the eating, so to mix my metaphor, I am not counting my chickens yet, though I do count two students absent from our class, and when I ask I am told they are "travelling." To be followed up on. Not less important, I have now asked the students to read James Baldwin's brilliant little essay "Equal in Paris," concerning the time when he "was arrested as a receiver of stolen goods and spent eight days in prison." We discuss it, first in what I used to call "small group discussions," but what are now, in the age of Zoom, called "Breakout Groups," in which the class is divided into two or more small groups which meet virtually so as to allow discussion among its members, after which we come together as a class again. What the students say when we meet is perceptive and to the point, but not engaged, by which I mean it really has nothing to do with they themselves, or with whatever they take to be the purpose and meaning of our class. I have brought James Baldwin into our discussion this semester because I thought it likely that a merely virtual encounter between tutors and learners would inhibit the kind of personal exchange, involving matters other than our texts, that I see when we meet together as a class. That better circumstance allowed many of our tutors to encounter difference face-to-face, and often to embrace it in a way that could lead to a way of feeling, and sometimes of knowing, things that went beyond a kind of loving sympathy. But not today.

Still, today is only our first taste of this good man, and we will see what tomorrow brings. I had hoped that it might move us beyond the easy American explanation of racism that is now, after the unspeakable murder of Mr. George Floyd, everywhere about us, to a less narrowly constructed explanation, one that takes into account wealth as well as race, and does not blink at the powerful role of class. In the end, I do not offer an answer to my questions, but simply call attention to the last words in the essay, Baldwin's reference to the superior and uncomprehending laughter of the powerful that at the end of all his suffering he hears in a French court, laughter that "is universal and can never be stilled."

September 30

And now time has passed, and it is suddenly the last day of September, and we are having an interesting discussion. Earlier in the class one perceptive tutor had pointed out that her young learner was being "overstimulated" by all the electronic devices to which, now living at home, she was being so regularly and unremittingly subjected: radios, TV, smart phones, tablets, pc's, even Raz-Kids. No wonder she runs about, as her tutor says she does. But the tutor also thinks that, in due course, she can manage what she has to, though she warns us, rightly I think, that there are no panaceas in what we are about, and that in some ways we are ourselves in danger of contributing to the confusing electronic blizzard that the pandemic has visited upon our so young learners.

October 5

Later we talk again about James Baldwin's essay, "Notes of a Native Son," from which the book in which it was included took its name. We move briefly into "Breakout Groups," and the students discuss the essay in virtual groups, before joining up into a class again. Among other things, we consider Baldwin's changes of attitude towards his father, from his childish (but so understandable) hatred, to a recognition not only of sympathy but even of love, to what we decide may be something else, a kind of empathy that forgives and asks forgiveness too. We ask, or I do, if we empathize with our learners, or only love and sympathize with them, understanding that the one has social, even political implications, while the other does not. It seems to me to take time, different in each case, and to last or not, often depending, among many things, upon the closeness of the bond. Towards the end of our discussion, one of our tutors says she had been called for a Teach for America interview, and when she mentioned the work she had been doing at Golden Rule, one of the judges had asked if she had been considering questions of race.

Such questions, by no means unfriendly, are not uncommon in such interviews, which often come from examiners who may entertain doubts about the pedagogical effectiveness of such efforts as our own, and so speak to the degree of social, or even political actualization that takes place, a topic which can be no less complicated. On the one hand, tutors expect that their work is going to inform them in more ways than pedagogical, and they entertain this expectation whether they have done such work in the past or not. But it is no less important that they not have this enlightenment (for want of a better word) handed to them, but that they achieve it themselves. Sometimes they do so, it seems to me, by setting present efforts over against those in the past, or perhaps against earlier influences, whether familial or other, or through simple reflection, one that may be informed by books. But if it is to last, it must come from within, and by no means be required by sudden precept. When we work, as we have for thirty years, face-to-face, I hardly use even good texts to see us through, since my hope is that many or most of our tutors will finally come to an understanding and agenda of their own. And now in virtual reality it still is that, though certainly James Baldwin will do no harm, and may even harden the resolve of one or all. But be it their discovery, not mine. In the end I ask if the question had been posed in a friendly way, and apparently it had been, so the questioner may once have done what we do, since our only irreconcilable critics tend to be those who have had little or no experience in the trenches.

October 19

During the twenty-seven years we were active at Sursum Corda, October was always my favorite month to work there, for what seemed to me many good reasons. First of all, by October most of our more difficult problems had been put to bed. The tutors and learners were finally assigned, were getting to know each other, and most of them now understood the perimeters of their interactions. Tutors had begun to see exactly where their learners were, and the best of them had already engaged previewing and predicting strategies for the young, followed by echo reading, voice pointing, and word sorts. Older learners, new or not, were, with luck, already beginning to respond to FIAT questions, and beginning to write a little, too. Our new learners had by then stopped pretending that they knew less than they did, and in a good year we had at least begun to discuss, in our mid-weekly learner-free seminar, not only our academic accomplishments (or shortcomings), but also what we were up to, and the possibility of an excursion, usually undertaken in groups of two, three or very occasionally four tutors, accompanying a like number of learners, or a slightly larger number, if an extra sibling or two got into the mix. But I have still a distinct memory, while riding down to Sursum Corda on cool October evenings, of feeling a certain relief when our books were in place, our drivers identified, and our tutors and learners beginning to interact. There is a Renoir film about the making of a film, in which he identifies the point in which the actors are present, things are at last in place, and work is going on. It is a time, he says, when "cinema is king." For me, that sensation came in October.

But nothing without change. Tutor and learner excursions have not been a part of our program at Golden Rule, whether because we are still new there, though less so every year, or because of some more active note of resistance, though whether from parents and care-givers, the authorities to whom we report, or from somewhere else, is hard to say. We have had group excursions to Georgetown from Golden Rule Apartments for the last two years, part of our strategy in ensuring that our learners, young as they are, know what a university is and that it's fun. We hope, of course, that the lesson will be recalled in time to come, when they are a few years older. These have been unfailingly successful: we (not me) run about a bit when we first arrive (not me), look at the cavernous and interesting classrooms in Healy, play a little (perhaps too briefly?) in a basketball court in the gym, have lunch usually in a student's dorm apartment, and return reluctantly, having promised that we'll surely come again.

There is none of that this year, of course, and that is one reason I am concerned that our tutorials not turn into drill sessions, even ones rooted in as good a program as Raz-Kids. But first of all, we (by whom I mean Bradley and myself) must know that Raz-Kids is being employed and understood by all who are going to use it, and that the role of comprehension on the tutor's part, as well as that of the learner is in operation, and that is why I insist on previewing, prediction, and the FIAT questions first of all.

An October Surprise

The difficulty with October, on the other hand, is that it is also the month in which tutors who are working well begin to know it. This is no bad thing in itself, and in many cases it can and will carry on throughout the semester. But in other cases, the tutor can become repetitious and even disengaged, and tend toward repeating what has worked in the past, instead of looking ahead. It's a failure I recognize in myself, at least sometimes, but academic that I am, spot it more easily in others. I sound this concern gently during an online class, but get no reaction. In the same session however, Bradley helpfully introduces a problem he has encountered, and that he diplomatically describes as "background conversations," that is, talk by others in the same room where the tutoring is taking place, and other noises as well, that inevitably intrude upon a tutorial. It is a problem, I believe, that other tutors have encountered as well, and one in particular has now addressed it, if not with Bradley's equanimity. Tutor and learner are not necessarily isolated as they were when we worked face-to-face, indeed in one recent session the learner's well-meaning mother took an active part in the tutorial, and remonstrated with her son when he did not respond quickly enough – in others, easily overheard arguments between and among siblings intrude too easily. If there is an easy answer to any of this we have yet to find it. But my sense remains that our tutors are generally most welcome into the familial mix, and though in one case this may not be entirely true, whether the tutor has not ingratiated himself sufficiently, or whether the family circumstances are against him, is quite unclear. In another case, we have three learners, each with her own tutor, sharing one tablet, or perhaps two. In a third there may possibly be no tablet present at all, although in this case the tutor involved has offered to help with finding one and connecting it, (but apparently, there may be one somewhere about after all). But he has not been allowed to do so, though his attempt to conduct his tutorial over the telephone has not, thus far, been notably successful.

These evident challenges have come upon us unannounced, after what had seemed to be an initial success, and beyond these more technical difficulties, one of our tutors has been having difficulty reengaging with his learner of last year as the semester has gone on. This may be my fault, as once the tutor/learner relationship was reestablished I had assumed that, as in the past, it would continue as begun. But our new arrangements now involve others in the household, the availability of electronic media, and the understandable disinclination on everyone's part – tutors, learners, care-givers – to call attention to difficulties. My past practice was simply to respect tutors while they were working, and to speak with them in private if I spotted something that needed change, unless it was something pressing, for example a too-difficult book. But the more serious difficulties (affecting three out of ten, a higher percentage than I had hoped), finally came clear when I spotted a silence and pressed the issue, and so discovered three missed tutorial appointments, only apparently caused by a problem with the Zoom. If I now understand what happened, difficulties were promised on the phone to be soon fixed, but never were, if they in fact existed. I reach out to Mr. Foster who has access to the apartments, and who very generously agrees to help if he can do so. Time will tell.

But if in the beginning I believed too easily that things would work themselves out, I am not sure that I should have been much more pushy than I was, though I might have asked more questions, and sooner, than I did. We come into our learners' homes at request (though usually our request, if truth be told), and when, for whatever reason, that request is refused we must quietly go away. The difficulty this time was that three students had learners assigned to them, who seemed, after a good beginning, to be working out. But it was not so. It transpires that they have not been able to develop or now even continue their connections, in spite of efforts on their part (they report that they call, arrange a session, but no one answers at the appointed hour) -- and we still have half of the semester to go. I am concerned, but probably should not be surprised. After more than a month, I have come to understand that, depending upon circumstances, even our virtual presence in an apartment can, depending upon the apartment's size and the number of persons involved, prove inconvenient, unlike earlier days, when our learners could simply be dispatched to our study rooms in the basement and so be out of the way for an hour or so.

So, it may have seemed sensible for parents and caregivers to agree to continue in the program into this semester too, to let the tutoring continue, not realizing that there would be new inconveniences for one and all, not all of them virtual. Still, the evidence seems to be that eight times out of eleven (counting Bradley, who is tutoring as well) these difficulties could be attended to, but not in the remaining three. For whatever reason, the call from the tutor goes unanswered, difficulties persist, and initially at least, the tutors have no idea what is going on. I will reach out again to Mr. Foster, to see is there is any possibility of reawakening interest with two of the three parents involved, and also to my former Sursum Corda contacts, in order to see if there is another learner to be found, but I have no great expectation of success. For now at least the die is cast, and that we have eight out of eleven ongoing sessions, and I am inclined to consider a success. But in this experiment of ours, I will now consider doubling up the remaining tutors, a practice we have resorted to in the past, almost always with good – indeed often with very good – results.

But I am reluctant to do so. Our program works best, I continue to insist, one-on-one, though over the years we often admitted variation, and I can still recall one excellent Sursum Corda tutor who in her last year with us would regularly collect together six quite young learners, who knew each other (and her) very well, and soon would not be taught by anyone else. Though I could see them, the tutor and her group were physically separated from the rest of us, and together held a most impressive little seminar, twice a week. What we face here, of course, is the opposite, but Bradley agrees with me that two tutors often make for a pedagogically effective mix, even when they have to share a learner between them, as happens sometimes when one learner is absent. He also reminds me what I had quite forgotten, that when he was in the program, and his learner had effectively vanished for a few weeks, he joined forces first with one colleague, then another, and the results pleased one and all. Their shared learner, he added, was quite chuffed to have the services of two tutors, and their pedagogy had been excellent, or so he says.

We talk it through, and subsequently Bradley agrees, having consulted with Malcolm, his own just-turned eight-year-old learner, to make room for one of the now learner-less young men. He agrees to work with Jack Lynch, the tutor who has just joined the program, and so has no experience before this semester. The two other tutors, James and Andrew, were with us last semester, and are both very able tutors, which suggests that their present difficulties are none of their doing, and makes the result all the more disappointing. I will soon bite the bullet and ask them to work with another tutor, I shall say, "at least for now," but will mean until the semester's end. Still, I continue to hope, against the odds, that another learner (or possibly even two) may one day soon appear. In the mean-time, I have every confidence that Bradley will prove not only an excellent tutor to Malcolm, but also our able colleague to Jack, and may they all, please God, learn from each other.

November 9
Beloved

We have been discussing what I take to be Toni Morrison's *magnum opus*, but doing so less easily than I had hoped, de-layed initially by the horrific event that is hidden, imperfectly and intentionally, at the book's center, and that comes to stand not only for the world of slavery itself, but also for what fol-lowed afterward. After a pause, I pitch my late friend Eusebio Rodrigues' description of the book as "an extended blues per-formance," as a way of addressing its unfamiliar, non-linear narrative, rooted in memory as it is, and of moving discussion beyond Sethe's murder of her infant, an historical event that, once learned, can never be forgotten. But that leads, through the character of *Beloved*, to the possibility, in the short third part, that Denver's entry into another world, one that reaches beyond memory, seems to offer, and to such forgiveness, after such knowledge, as may one day come about. In saying so I may be offering a kind of imperfect apologia for the work we do, and I understand that some will find such an explanation unconvincing, even offensive, since we cannot, of course, compensate for what we acknowledge, only admit it. But ideological purity has its own limitations, and good intention, however imperfect, is not to be despised. Literature sometimes encourages us not only to think and to judge, but also to live more wisely and to love with greater generosity, and it can do so even in the worst of times, in the times of *Beloved* and of George Floyd, among young and old alike.

At Work: November 20

For some weeks now, and in spite of the difficulties I have described, tutoring has been going well, and more or less as planned. Two of the groups of three (two tutors, one learner) have worked out as well as I could have wished; the third (ahem) has yet to come together. Malcolm and Darrius, isolated in their homes, were delighted to have another tutor added to their group, and after an initial period of introduction, explanation, and adjustment, have taken to their work again with what I am told is evident pleasure, though those were not the words used, posing questions as well as answering them, a practice I have been trying to encourage, in my own classes as well. This arrangement is not one I had either planned for or particularly welcomed, but this has been a semester of unexpected developments, and I must not snatch defeat from victory. Even so, I somewhat fear that I may have announced our success too soon. There was less of a danger of my doing so when we were teaching face-to-face, and I was an attentive though (generally) unobtrusive presence at most of our meetings. But throughout this semester tutor and learner have been working virtually and alone, and I find myself acquiescing perhaps too uncritically in such reports as come my way, well-meaning though they are. Will it happen one day, should such tutorials as we are experimenting with contain more than eleven pairs, that they will be discreetly recorded or otherwise observed, and any uncertainty resolved? Perhaps, but not too soon, I hope. My belief remains that such teaching as we undertake cannot be readily scripted. Even as we teach each other, we converse about examples, not models, as I do in what I am writing here and now. For us, there is no single model that will satisfy, nor any short cut, finally, to the experience, dear in both senses, through which we learn.

Even so, when I touched on this difficulty with Bradley a few weeks ago, he offered that, after a string of good tutorials indeed, he had had one that was less so, and offered to describe it to our class. This he does almost too effectively, excellent tutor that he is, with rather more self-deprecation than was necessary, but to good effect. He begins by acknowledging that he was tired when he began to teach, and so failed to "bring my all" to his tutorial, or really to set the tone for what was to follow. He ended by allowing that even Malcolm, his young learner, felt something was amiss, and asked to end the session early – which he never does. This brought forth a degree of candor from our best tutors, one of whom reported what sometimes happens when there are three learners and only one tablet, another indicated the baleful influence the telephone can have on concentration. But then a third summarized what seemed to be a general conclusion, that the greatest challenge in virtual tutoring is maintaining not so much attention as focus, and all agree that while this difficulty is not entirely absent from tutoring face-to-face either, it is at once more present, pressing, and less easily contained when tutoring online, and is something every tutor will confront. To my delight, we then turn to poetry again, and two of the more conscientious tutors read to the rest of us their learners' latest raps.

November 30

But now the end of the semester has appeared on the horizon, and it will be upon us all too soon, and we must begin to consider what we may have accomplished in so short a time. One intervention in two of our groups recently emerged when family members other than the learner joined in with the tutorial, mostly uninvited. The tutors seemed initially to have been a little nonplused, even a little defensive, by this development, but rightly played along, and things went well. In one case the intruder was a well-meaning brother two or four years older than the learner, who simply wanted to take part as well, even to help, and it would have been bad manners to try to push him away. The added presence worked out particularly well when the session turned to dramatic reading, and each one could take a separate role. It soon became apparent that the brother was hardly ever present, and seemed to live elsewhere. But his presence was especially welcome to his younger sister, and the tutorial allowed him to speak to and interact with her, in a way she much welcomed. This sort of happy meeting is unique to our present circumstances, and would not have come about when we were still meeting downstairs, and working one-on-one. In another case, and not for the first time, a mother intervened again, helpfully at first, but then she again became irritated when her son read too slowly, and unhelpfully remonstrated with him.

Otherwise things proceed as they have been, and Izzy (I think it was) points out that when things are going well there is less to report, FIAT questions apart, than when there is an interruption or a problem of some sort. I agree, and what she says brings back to me something a former and very excellent Dean of the College, Fr. Roydon B. Davis, S.J., once said, that universities work as they should, and education proceeds best of all, when things are generally as they should be, and distractions are as few as possible.

December 2

There is a story in today's *Washington Post* that might almost serve as a coda for our program. In it, Perry Stein reports the way the pandemic has impacted the reading progress of many D.C. students. An internal headline summarizes his argument: "In first grade, 90% hit reading target. In second, none did." The piece reminded me that from the beginning, over thirty years ago at Sursum Corda, and now three years ago at Golden Rule, encouragement in reading and the language arts have been the bread and butter of our program. And this past semester in particular, our young learners have welcomed into their familial orbit not only their tutor, but when necessity compelled it, their tutor's colleague too, rightly understanding that both had come to smooth and speed the way.

So it was that, at our final seminar, with the easy nonchalance of the young, and after sounding once again our now-familiar themes, the tutors said goodbye to Bradley and myself, and we to them, and like many who have come before, they set out to grow, in time, in wisdom, and in grace.

Coming to an End: December 7

I have not written much, in what has come before, about one salient feature of our programs, both formerly at Sursum Corda and now at Golden Rule Apartments, that needs a word, and that is the circumstance that most of our learners are Black, most of our tutors White. This state of things, to be sure, came about not at all by choice, and it is almost invariable that many of our very best tutors are Black, both men and women, and act as a welcome model not only to their own young learners, but to others in the program as well. Seeking to add to their number, I have sometimes raised my concern for this evident reality with such tutors as I thought would respond to it, and those conversations evoked a variety of responses, almost all of them quite true. First of all usually comes the fact that the requirements of Georgetown's curriculum, and those of individual majors, do not leave many openings for such courses as my own; then the fact that many students have not heard of the program or the class, and some that have done are put off because so many of the tutors are White. But one student I spoke to recently added this explanation to the others: that it can be difficult for some Black students, who themselves will have already suffered from evident racism, to believe themselves now in a position from which they can and should promote deeper entry into a culture that is itself far from equitable and just. But others, he added, like himself, certainly are willing to act and to join in spite of what experience has taught them, or in response, he thought, to what a different experience, or common sense, or a mentor, may have taught them. But really, he thought, in the end the reasons are as different as those who, like he himself, do take part, or like others, who don't.

To all of this I have no easy answer, and if I address it at all, I can only do so by reaching out to one of my own heroes, the Rev. Dr. Martin Luther King, Jr., who famously welcomed White people into his own great project when others did not, and who did so because he believed that ethics and morality were not the property of any group alone, rightly insisting in his 1963 "Letter from Birmingham Jail," that "injustice anywhere is a threat to justice everywhere." He went on, in that extraordinary document, to offer that belief as a way of accounting for and defending the "direct action" his followers were then taking, while also representing himself as "gravely disappointed" with those White moderates who claimed to endorse his ends, without equally supporting what was necessary to bring them about. I understand of course that our "direct action," which is what, changes having been made, I take our program to represent, is not precisely what Dr. King had in mind, but even so I venture to cite our work as a way of seeking admission into his continuing agenda, and dare to echo, if with an echo of Chaucer's farewell, his great and final words from Birmingham. Thus, if our work, imperfect as it is, has inclined tutor and learner toward a cultural, as well as an academic literacy, one that inclines towards civility, equality, and justice, then I thank therefore tutor and learner alike, and also all of those who sped us on our way, from parents and caregivers to deans and administrators, and to those at Sursum Corda and at Golden Rule who always had our back. And if, while working together, we realized in our meetings, however briefly, however imperfectly, and in spite of an occasional squabble, even a fraction of that brotherhood and sisterhood we always sought, then for that fellowship I thank the same God whom we all acknowledge, in whatever way we do, for that great and lasting blessing.

Chapter 7

Zoom Calls About Nothing and Everything

By Bradley Galvin, M.A.

Introduction

During the fall of 2020, as the world turned towards virtual learning amidst a global pandemic, a new frontier awaited the long-standing Community-Based Learning (CBL) course, Sursum Corda. Typically, this CBL course operates in partnership with the residents of Golden Rule Apartments and pairs Georgetown students with learners between the ages of 6-12 to engage in a one-on-one relationship around literacy tutorials twice a week. These tutorials operated out of the community room at Golden Rule Apartments, something that would become impossible in the fall of 2020, due to safety and health concerns for both the residents at Golden Rule and Georgetown students. Instead, the Georgetown students and their learners adapted to a virtual interface to conduct their tutorials and formed, or in some cases, maintained, relationships with each other. To do so, learners and tutors would log onto a Zoom conference, typically set up by the tutor and the learner's caregiver, with the tutor sharing their screen to show the virtual reading software of their choice. One of the main virtual reading softwares used by tutors was Raz-Kids, graciously provided by the Director of the Red House and Vice Provost, Randy Bass. This reading software was suggested by former Community Director at Golden Rule, Patrick Williams. It provides the learner with a customized interactive learning environment centered on reading books and completing comprehension quizzes to receive points to be spent on the learner's robot avatar within the software. Other softwares used by tutors include Scribd and Arcedmics. The tutorials would typically be held twice a week for an hour, at times mutually agreed upon between tutor and learner.

While the world of virtual service learning is not entirely new, it has seen rapid growth as a result of the remote learning environment forced upon students worldwide. The CBL course, Sursum Corda, was proud to have contributed to this growth and has gained tremendous insight through first-hand participation. What drove this for "Virtual Sursum Corda" last fall was the simple question of the viability of virtual service learning. However, this comes with a subset of categories that derive from the examination of virtual learning and relationships. In terms of the viability of virtual service learning on behalf of the learners, this includes an engagement with the reading material, the ability to maintain attention, and enjoyment of the time spent with the tutor. In the case of the tutors, this meant creating or maintaining relationships with their learners on a virtual interface, the ability to provide academic as well as emotional support for their learners, and engagement with the reflection of work done and time spent with their learners. These factors would be measured three main ways: on surveys given to learners; the reflection journals and papers written by the tutors; and quantitative data from Raz-Kids on the learning progress of the learners. Of course, each particular case was highly dependent on various factors, including internet capacity for learners and tutors, accessibility of internet for learners, and the status of the relationship between learner and tutor going into the semester. In addition, this report examines the successes and limitations of virtual service learning for the Sursum Corda course. This includes the reliability and validity of our virtual service learning this semester, and how our work can contribute to the assessment of education during COVID-19 and remote learning more broadly. What follows is my account of the relationship I built with my learner, named Malcolm (8) in this text for sake of privacy. It will provide first-hand insight into the virtual service work conducted this semester. Afterwards, I will examine this account and more broadly discuss the experiences of the class as a whole as we answer the questions outlined previously.

9/15/20 - First Call with Learner's Mother

Finally! Today I connected with Malcolm's mother on the phone after many failed attempts over the past few weeks. It is essential to include and engage the parent in the child's learning, and I am glad I called Malcolm's mom before reaching out to him to build more trust in the relationship. As the conversation progressed, I could feel her getting more and more comfortable talking to me. One of the biggest positives to come out of the conversation for me was my learning that both Malcolm and his mother were familiar with the two softwares we will be using this fall: the video conferencing platform Zoom, and the online reading software Raz-Kids. This will be a huge benefit once we start conducting the tutoring sessions.

After my conversation with Malcolm's mother, I went over to my sister, who works in finance, to tell her about the great news. She was happy for me, but immediately said that I needed to be more professional on the phone when conducting work calls. I replied that she is working in a completely different sphere than I, and colloquial language tends to be more beneficial when communicating with the people with whom I work. I believe that it allows for more authenticity, which ultimately leads to more trust. However, I do need to pay attention to the type of language I use with my co-workers, as there is a distinction between work and everyday life.

I still stand by my belief that speaking authentically is crucial for building trust in my work, but I will make sure to bring increased awareness around my language.

9/21/20 - First Session

What an amazing first tutoring session!! That could not have gone any better! Malcolm is such a curious and sweet kid. I could tell that my goofy virtual background of a cross-eyed lama in Machu Pichu quickly put him at ease and made him excited to learn with me. His prior knowledge of Raz-Kids certainly helped facilitate the session. I felt like I could get to every level of FIAT (Factual, Interpretative, Applicative, Transactive) questions quickly, which is something I found to be difficult in person during my time in the Sursum Corda course as an undergraduate. What definitely makes a difference from my previous experience as an undergrad tutor in the program is Malcolm's young and enthusiastic age compared to my previous learner, who was a few years older. This likely had an impact on Malcolm's ability to trust me so quickly.

The most insightful part of the tutoring session was the fact that we were conducting the session from Malcolm's home, rather than in person in the community room, as was always done in the past. With this change of environment, I got a raw glimpse into his home life that I was never afforded during my previous work in person. This opens up a whole array of ethical and academic questions as to how this changes the relationship.

9/28/20

At the start of today's session, I could tell Malcolm was burnt out from school. When I caught up with him about his weekend, he couldn't stop moving. From the couch to the floor, back to the couch. It reminded me of when I would get home from school as a kid and climb on top of the table to lie down and shut out the world for a little bit. The last thing I wanted to do was talk about anything resembling school when I was in that mood. Knowing this, I decided to direct Malcolm's energy elsewhere, and taught him how to change his background on Zoom, since he loves seeing which one I show up with to our tutoring sessions. The first thing he changed it to was a mask of Spider-Man so he could fit his head in the cutout and become Spider-Man—I mean, how could you not want to be Spider-Man?? After that, he changed his background to a picture of his family at his parents' wedding. He pointed to each person and told me their names. Thus, I was officially "introduced" to his family.

It felt pretty amazing that Malcolm was ready and excited to introduce me to his family, if only through a photograph, after meeting together three times virtually. I honestly believe the isolation caused by this pandemic has made people long for social interactions. This makes interactions more meaningful, even if they're only virtual. After a few minutes of having fun with our virtual backgrounds, Malcolm and I were ready to get back to Raz-Kids, to continue our quest to read books, in order to purchase a space chimp for our Raz Rocket by reading books. Fun tools and achievements in the Raz-Kids software help incentivize curious young learners like Malcolm.

10/2/20

Another dimension of virtual learning beginning to emerge is conversational background noises. This is exactly what I was alluding to earlier about the new set of ethical questions that come with working virtually in their homes, rather than in person in the community room as in the past. In some ways, it can be seen as an invasion of privacy, and at the same time, could also signify a significant level of trust on behalf of the residents of Golden Rule towards Georgetown. A big question mark is whether or not Malcolm's family realizes that I can hear some of what they're saying in the background. For the most part, it's indistinguishable. Half the time it's the TV, and the other half, it's people talking. At one point, I could hear Malcolm's mother mention my name in conversation, but I couldn't tell what she said. At another point, I could listen to what I presumed to be Malcolm's father talking about someone being held up at gunpoint, reminding me what different worlds Malcolm and I live in. Maybe I should let them know in some way. I do have my learner's mother's number.

Another theme I am starting to pick up on is what kinds of books Malcolm chooses to read. Typically, he chooses books about nature and animals, often in amazement of the pictures that accompany the story. Malcolm alludes to how he has not encountered much outside of DC. This is also reflected in his heightened interest in reading. One of the books we read this time was about the life of George Washington. Included in the story was a reference to the slaves owned by the family, referred to in the book as "Stablemen." Malcolm didn't say anything about it, so I decided not to get into it. While it could have been a deep conversation, I feel that Malcolm is a little young. But who am I to say, especially as a young White man.

Throughout our session, Malcolm continued to count down the time we had left. "40 more minutes...30 more minutes...20...," he said. For a while, I assumed it was because he was bored and couldn't wait for our session to end. That's how I used to think when I was getting tutored as a child. But I could not have been more wrong. As the minutes started to wane, Malcolm grew more and more anxious, eventually revealing he was sad that we only had a few more minutes left. I was deeply touched, and ashamed for making my assumption. Growing up, I definitely did not appreciate my tutors as Malcolm does. I guess that goes to show the privilege I had growing up, seeing tutoring as extra work and not an opportunity. The moment was definitely another reality check. The highlight of the night came at the end when Malcolm called me his friend when saying goodbye. It is wonderfully unique how we have cultivated this relationship so quickly without having met each other in person.

10/9/20

After last week's session, I continued to think about how Malcolm and I have cultivated this relationship so quickly through a virtual interface. I believe that the pandemic plays a massive role in our ability to build this relationship and trust despite never having met. In general, I can feel people desperate to connect these days, having been confined to their homes for so long.

While reading a book about ponds with my learner, a precious moment came about. One of the critters mentioned in the book was a Whirligig Beetle. Naturally, Whirligig became my new favorite word because of how ridiculous it sounds. When I proclaimed that it was my new favorite word, Malcolm said that he had never had a favorite word before and wanted to find one of his own. Once we transitioned to a modern Latino take on the story of Cinderella called *Cinderello*, his favorite word quickly became Jose (the protagonist). In that moment, I could feel the program and my personality rubbing off on Malcolm simultaneously.

This week's big moment came when Malcolm revealed that he had read all of the books for school that we had been reading previously in our tutorial sessions. I should have realized this earlier, given the fact that Malcolm uses Raz-Kids for school and immediately knew his reading level. On the one hand, he tricked me into doing less work. On the other hand, this also indicates he just loves spending time with me no matter what we were reading. I was genuinely surprised that Malcolm had already read all of our books based on his enthusiasm for reading. The amount of laughter and smiles we have each week lets me know that our relationship means a lot to Malcolm; I know it means a lot to me.

10/16/20

After learning we have been reading books that Malcolm has already read, I decided to increase the reading level on Raz-Kids to give Malcolm new and more challenging books. The quizzes on this level are far more difficult and should keep Malcolm even more engaged than he already is.

The first book that we read on this level was about Rosa Parks, which opened up a conversation between Malcolm and me about the ongoing social movement, Black Lives Matter. At one point while reading the book, Malcolm said that now-adays Black people and White people like each other, unlike in the book. I replied that while that should be the case, there is still a lot of work to be done in our society. While I didn't want to crush his blissful ignorance, I did feel it was important to be honest with Malcolm. In return, Malcolm opened up about what was happening with Black Lives Matter, saying that what's happening to Black people is crazy. However, this was immediately followed by Malcolm stating that he just loves playing, confirming my notion that he is a little young to be engaged in these issues. Then again, as Tahneheisi Coates points out in his book *Between the World and Me*, Malcolm will eventually have to take on the most difficult task of being a Black man in America and should not be lied to about the rough path ahead of him.

We followed the book on Rosa Parks with a much light-er read: *Dogs at Work*. Frankly, it astonishes me what dogs are able to do. One of the dog jobs we read about had to do with water rescue missions off the coast of the Gulf of Mexico. This, of course, diverted into a conversation about the superhero Aquaman, which led me to ask Malcolm who his favorite superhero is. He replied Tony Stark and Batman, because they're rich. I tried to impart on Malcolm that money isn't everything and that it's more important to be kind to others.

10/19/20

Tonight, Malcolm wasn't feeling particularly well, so I decided to take it easy. We began by just catching up about his weekend, with him telling me about the fun he had spending time at his grandmother's. To my delight, Malcolm was also interested in what was going on in my life. I told him about the fun I had had with my friends and father watching football all Sunday at his place. I think Malcolm was surprised to learn that my parents did not live together. I wonder if this was unfamiliar to him, given the fact that his parents are still married. In any case, I'm glad I was able to share this part of my identity with him, as it makes up so much of who I am today. However, I did not get into my depression with him. I felt again he may be too young to talk about something like that. At the same time, though, I also want to be open about my struggles, so he can feel comfortable talking to me if he ever feels similar. I can hear his parents fighting or yelling in the background sometimes and know how much that took a toll on me when I was his age.

In addition to Malcolm's physical and mental fatigue from remote learning, there has definitely been an emotional fatigue from not being able to be with his classmates. Malcolm clearly misses school, especially spending time with friends. Apparently, only one of his friends from school lives in his building. I can't imagine how tough it is to be that young during this pandemic. All my days growing up were spent playing with friends and cultivating memories. Social interactions are so critical at his age, and I am so sorry for Malcolm and all the other children right now who are being robbed of their childhood by this pandemic.

Oh yeah ...WE'RE STILL READING BOOKS MALCOLM ALREADY READ! Part of me wants to make sure he is being honest, but I can also tell that Malcom's deception comes out of a need to play. I was not so different from Malcolm when I was his age. In fact, I can recall failing my first-grade reading test on purpose just so I could get the easy books. My mom found out not too long after I came home with a one-word page book that consisted of a picture of a cow and a caption of "Cow." It took only a day longer until my mom came into school and explained to my teacher, "HE CAN READ!"

10/23/20

During our weekly in-class discussion with the other tutors, Professor Hirsh reminded me of the importance of re-reading, something I've never honestly done before. As a child, I was completely opposed to anything that had to do with reading or writing. In my childish mind, there was no point to reading a novel like *Lord of the Rings*, which would take me months, when I could watch the whole series on television in a day. But as I've tried to return to some of my childhood hobbies during this pandemic -- skateboarding in the driveway and playing guitar at night -- I am reminded of the importance of repetition and discipline. So what if Malcolm has already read the books we've been reading?? The important thing is the practice and comprehension that comes with reading, and Malcolm has succeeded with both.

　　This new reading level we have entered in Raz-Kids is much more difficult than what we have dealt with previously. The questions for the comprehension quizzes are three times as long and resemble a standardized test. At one point during the quiz, I explained to Malcolm what "All of the above" meant, and I was happy to add this to his vernacular at such a young age. I am glad he is being exposed to questions he will face in future pivotal exams, but the format and rhetoric used at this level brought a sense of engagement that reminded Malcolm of school. The atmosphere at this level removed the joy from our lesson and placed Malcolm in the last place he wanted to be at our hour together -- school.

10/26/20

In order to utilize this virtual learning space more during my tutorials, tonight I incorporated videos connected to our reading throughout. This idea was brought to me by another tutor/friend in the program. He had found great success in raising his learner's engagement in the readings by seamlessly weaving in videos connected to their books.

It was fairly easy to try out this new learning technique tonight, because our reading was about the largest vehicles in the world. I mean, who doesn't want to see a giant crane in action? I was very careful in selecting the videos to watch, making sure that they came from a verified account, identified by the check mark next to the account name on YouTube, so that no inappropriate videos would accidentally show up.

While watching a video about the amphibious duck boat, I mentioned to Malcolm in passing that I used to make videos in college. This blew him away, and he immediately asked to see one of my films. I decided to show him the first documentary I made about the brutal Italian sport of Calcio Historico during my time studying abroad in Florence. Malcolm had never heard of Italy before and was mesmerized by its beauty while watching the film. He had also never heard of documentaries before, so I was thrilled to be able to introduce them to him, as they were such a large source of my learning as a child due to my thirst for film and knowledge.

11/2/20

Tonight, I will be joining forces with another tutor in the class whose learner has unfortunately decided to drop out of the Sursum Corda program. I'm very interested to see how the presence of a second tutor affects the tutorials with my learner. My immediate reaction when Professor Hirsh asked if I would take on another tutor was concern; I thought it might make the interaction between Malcolm and me less significant and our tutorials would start to feel more like school than a developing meaningful relationship between two individuals. On the flip side, it could also make Malcolm even more engaged and excited to learn with another new friend in the "room." He did seem excited when I brought up the idea to him last week.

Thank God, it turned out to be the latter. Malcolm was thrilled to have another person with whom to interact and learn. He could barely contain his excitement throughout the tutorial, literally throwing himself against the couch out of pure joy. After I let Malcolm run around for a little to get his excitement out, the three of us began reading a book about China. At first, I took the lead in the tutorial, to help give the other tutor an idea of how we typically run our sessions. He did a good job slowly integrating himself into the tutorial, and even used some FIAT questions, which I'm sure will make Professor Hirsh happy. Malcolm was still goofy and playful throughout the reading of the book; however, he was able to retain almost all of the information, as was indicated by his perfect quiz score at the end.

As I have mentioned earlier, I think the biggest service we are providing Malcolm at this time is the added interaction and attention in his otherwise isolated life during this pandemic. Having an extra tutor in the session only aided in this regard. I look forward to continued success with the three of us working together.

11/9/20

Tonight was without a doubt the worst session that we have had. Coming into the session, I was exhausted from working all day. I could tell that the other tutor with whom I now work felt the same from the tired look on his face. Also, he was being constantly distracted by his phone. However, low energy is no excuse for a bad tutorial -- at least not on our end. As we worked through our tutorial, our low energy levels started rubbing off on Malcolm. At first, he was frustrated, and tried getting our attention by using the "draw on the screen" function for Zoom on iPads, as well as making funny faces. Neither of us tutors playfully engaged, as we usually do with this goofiness. This made Malcolm frustrated and by the end, he turned his video off and said he was tired and wanted to finish early. This was a first.

The students we serve deserve our full energy and attention while we work and engage with them, this year especially. The education that they are receiving online during this pandemic is nowhere near the necessary instruction children need and deserve. Not only that, these children are suffering emotionally, not being able to play with others and live the social life of a child. Instead, they're locked away in their rooms to keep them safe. Our extra support and attention are needed now more than ever, and this fact must not be forgotten.

11/16/20

This session was much better right off the bat. I actively used my sense of humor throughout the session, using funny voices and making witty comments about our book, *Goldilocks and the Other Three Bears*. Setting a lighthearted and playful tone made a big difference for both Malcolm and the other tutor with whom we work. I think the levity of the session made our time together feel less like school and more like time with friends. As a result, everyone was more engaged and free-flowing.

Malcolm wanted to end our session early again, however,

I could tell that he was truly exhausted from a day glued to the computer for school. In order to make the most of our time together, I incentivized Malcolm, saying that we could end early if he got a hundred percent on his comprehension quiz, which he did. I honestly would have ended the session early either way. "Zoom fatigue," as it's come to be known in this Covid age, is a real occurrence that I experience daily myself. I'm not a neuroscientist, but the amount of time we all spend on screens these days cannot be good. At the end of each day, I feel drained emotionally and physically, having sat in "virtually" (pun intended) the same spot staring at my computer screen for the entire day. I can only imagine what that must be like at eight years old.

11/20/20

Tonight was one of our most revealing sessions yet. The other tutor was unable to come tonight due to Covid issues at his place in DC. Regardless, Malcolm was clearly hurt by him not showing up to our session. I jokingly asked if I was no longer enough for him, to which he responded "No." However, I knew that was not what this was about. Malcolm has come to rely on our sessions for an outlet, and not having that full outlet made him feel let down. In turn, he wanted to end our session early, but I refused to give up.

Halfway through our session, my family came home from dinner, including my aunt and grandmother, who were visiting. Malcolm could hear their entrance through our Zoom call and asked if he could meet them. Seeing as I have met his family virtually, I felt it was only right to introduce him to mine. My family was incredibly excited to meet Malcolm, and vice versa. After spending some time with my family and Malcolm, I was reminded how important family is to the two of us. Malcolm is always proud to dawn on his background of his family during our sessions and is even more excited to hear my interest in them. He has definitely made me reflect on the importance of family in my own life. Family has always been a tricky subject for me. While there is so much laughter and joy, there is always great pain. It has taken me a long time to reconcile with my parents' divorce, and only now do I think I have come to a place of contentment, being blessed with this extra time with family due to these unprecedented times. At the end of the day, our parents are human, and a lot more like us than we ever dare to admit.

12/11/20 - Last Session

Unfortunately, the other tutor was unable to join Malcolm and me tonight due to finals; however, this turned out to be a blessing in disguise. At the start of the session, I could tell that Malcolm was in an exhausted state, as was I. At this time of year, it's difficult to focus on anything, while at the same time, everything is due. All I want to do during the Holidays is spend time with family and friends, and I know Malcolm feels the same. With this in mind, I felt our time together would be best spent simply talking and hanging out with each other, and boy, was I right!

Candidly put, sometimes I think I still have the mindset of a child, despite currently dawning the first legitimate form of facial hair I've ever known. I find it difficult to have "sophisticated conversations" with people my age and up. All I really care about is talking about the strange parts of life with people, and hopefully sharing a laugh or two. Part of what draws me to working with young learners is I find this to be much easier with those younger than I than with those around my age who are now trying to be taken "seriously" as an adult. "Serious" is overrated; helping others and having fun with those around you is much more important and satisfying for me. Without a doubt, this attitude stems from my parents who have miraculously been able to maintain their joyful disposition in life.

Tonight, the conversation between Malcolm and me sprung out of a debate on the largest animals of the ocean. I felt pretty confident that it was the blue whale, but Malcom was sure that it was not. Upon some digging, we discovered that the blue whale is indeed the largest, but the siphonophores is the longest (say that fish five time fast.) So we decided to call it a draw. After our ocean debate, my dog Bob started demanding attention from me. I introduced Malcolm to Bob, and he immediately picked up on Bob's coveted nickname, "Big Baby." I proceeded to hand Bob off to my biracial friend Yannik, who was visiting for a mini-vacation after being cooped up in his Jersey City apartment these past few months. Malcolm was excited to see someone on my screen who also looked like him, leading us to talk about race, if only at a surface level.

Yannik and I became friends at Georgetown when Yannik was a senior and I was a freshman. The two of us were introduced through a mutual friend and hit it off immediately because of our shared sense of humor. Yannik was my first close friend who was Black, and for a long time I didn't think much of it. More recently, however, race and racial relations have been at the top of my mind, given my field of studies in Education, work in social justice, and the national awakening around our country's history with slavery.

Race was something I hardly thought about growing up, due to my sheltered upbringing in a nearly homogeneous White, wealthy neighborhood in Greenwich, CT. It wasn't until I got to Georgetown as an undergraduate that I began becoming socially aware on issues of race and class, having been plucked out of my isolated pond in Connecticut. This really took root in the work I began doing in education as an undergrad, starting the summer after my freshman year. That summer I worked in a KIPP charter school in Bronx, NY, as a teacher's assistant. One moment in particular sparked my journey down a path towards social justice: one day, while I was helping sort through the mail, one of the middle-school-ers came into the admissions office and asked for his mid-day snack. My boss happily supplied the boy with a packet of gold fish, and the student went on his way. After the boy left, my boss explained to me that some of the students at the school were food insecure and would have trouble focusing during class due to hunger. Driving home that afternoon, I thought back to when I was in middle school and had similar prob-lems focusing due to my depression, caused by my parents' divorce when I was nine. I then thought to myself, "Imagine throwing hunger on top of your depression. No way someone could focus!" Yet this was what a lot of my students at KIPP had to cope with, as many came from broken homes and un-stable financial backgrounds.

This one moment of clarity sent me on a path of reflection that I have carried with me ever since. It ultimately lead me to this wonderful virtual learning experiment that may possibly become something much larger down the line, with my long term goal of helping to connect Georgetown students and the descendants of the 272 enslaved people sold by Georgetown University in 1838 to Maringouin, Louisiana. A project I have been blessed to be a part of thus far, all thanks to the friend-ship I've developed with the project's original founder, Jessi-ca "Milly" Tilson, a member of the Maringouin and larger GU 272+ descendant community.

While I don't know what will happen with the virtual tu-toring program in Louisiana at this point, I do know a few things from this little experiment of ours this semester. Peo-ple can form meaningful relationships and bonds through a virtual interface. While I may have been secretly skeptical at the beginning of this project, I am proudly convinced from the relationship I have formed with Malcolm. And while two individuals, and sometimes three, logging on from different parts of the world, from completely different racial and so-cio-economic backgrounds won't fix all the societal problems we confront today, it brings us to the greatest place to start--conversations about nothing and everything.

Evaluation/Main Takeaways

Following my last tutorial with Malcolm, I conducted a short survey with him to hear from his point of view how the semester went. Seeing that we are a Community Based Learning Course, it seemed only right to include the community's perspective in evaluating the semester. This survey consisted of 4 questions on a scale from one to five, with five being the best --

1) Did you like and enjoy the program?
2) Did you like Raz-Kids?
3) Did you like and have fun with your tutor?
4) Could you pay attention while you were working with your tutor?

-- to which Malcolm replied an astonishing and flattering "5 billion" for each question! However, while conducting the survey, Malcolm's mother overheard the questions and answers, and interjected on question four. She said that while Malcolm does a good job paying attention with his tutors, school is a completely different story. This was something that was consistent across the board for all the learners in the program, as indicated by the feedback provided from the other tutors' essays.

What became evident throughout the semester was the difficulty for our learners to maintain their attention when tutorials began to have a more rigid and "school-like feel." In analyzing the data provided by Raz-Kids, the areas in which our learners scored the highest on their comprehension quizzes came in categories revolving around big picture ideas and the ability to draw inferences and conclusions. This can be contributed to the long-standing motto and tools of the Sursum Corda Program that focus on comprehension. Where the learners tended to struggle more came in categories associated with skills such as "fact or opinion" or "compare and contrast," which are more closely tied with questions found on standardized tests. The struggle of remote learning is only harder when it becomes a task, which is often what testing feels like for young learners. At the heart of our program is the relationship between tutors and learners, and this cannot be compromised for the sake of advancement of proficiency in literacy and testing. In order to help our learners succeed in the classroom, our goal is to instill a love of learning and reading, which can easily be lost when tutorials lack their element of levity.

Another theme that emerged in relation to the difficulties of remote learning, and one where our program can help lessen the learning gap acquired by our learners' being removed from the classroom this year, was our learners' need for additional support in areas outside of literacy. At the end of the survey conducted with our learners, we left one open-ended question for the learners' caregivers, asking for any suggestions for the future. The only suggestion that was provided by my learner's mother was help with schoolwork in areas outside of reading, Spanish in particular. This was also seen in other tutors' work with their learners, in which they were asked to focus on other areas by either their learner or their caregiver.

One of the biggest successes for our virtual Sursum Corda experiment this semester was the tutors' ability to adapt to meet the needs of their learners' learning styles. While we came into this semester with a somewhat clear idea of how tutorials would run using Zoom and Raz-Kids, this was not ideal for every learner. For one, Raz-Kids tends to lean toward a younger demographic with its simplistic and childlike interface. For our older learners, this could feel demeaning and belittling. The most successful instances of not using Raz-Kids came from tutors with older learners; these older learners were encouraged to write and read poetry. In doing so, the tutorials began to instill a sense of ownership for their learners by having them create something of their own.

On the flip side, one of the biggest challenges of the semester came from coordinating tutorials with learners and their caregivers. This challenge crept up in several of my sessions with Malcolm, when I would either be waiting in limbo for over a half hour until he would log on, or the session would be canceled at the very last minute. This was something many of the other tutors encountered as well. In a couple of instances, learners in the program eventually dropped out after the tutor was unable to setup a consistent schedule with the learner's caregiver. The advantage of having tutorials conducted in person, in the same place at the same time each week, cannot be understated. In addition, an element that I believe needs to be further addressed and explored is the conversational background noises overheard by tutors. Whether or not the learner's family knows they can be overheard is unknown, and it is important that this be addressed for the sake of and respect for their own privacy.

With regard to the reliability and validity of our experiment, I believe that both are intertwined with the relationship of tutor and learner. There is no one-size-fits-all model that can be applied to virtual service learning. If this time of remote learning has taught us anything, it is that we need to be adaptive. Every child learns in a different manner, and every child needs support in different ways. Where the reliability of our experiment comes into question stems from the ability of each participant to conduct tutorials. For the learners, this can come from access to internet, devices, and suitable learning environments. In the case of the tutors, it comes from an understanding of proper pedagogy involved in service learning (virtual or in-person), ability to problem solve, and competency with the technology used in tutorials. However, what is undeniably reliable and valid about our experiment is the ability to build and maintain relationships strictly through a virtual interface, something that I am proud to say from first-hand experience.

Endnote: A Second Spring

I had intended to end this book with the chapter on what we managed to accomplish during the first semester of the pandemic, followed by my colleague's good description of his tutorials. I thought the second semester under lockdown would continue along the same lines as the first, and indeed it did, though with a development toward the end I had not anticipated.

In the beginning, thanks to the excellent help we had from our associate Mr. William Foster at Golden Rule Apartments, everything seemed to be going more or less as intended, and though we had to add several new tutors to replace those who had graduated or were otherwise unavailable, they proved without exception to be smart, quick to learn, and soon committed to their learners. But as the semester wore on, and especially as we approached the end of it, everyone needed to stop and take a breath. Sometimes the issue was finding a semi-quiet place in which to work. More than once, the tub in the bathroom became that place; under the bed was another.

Throughout the semester, the ability of the tutors to pose FIAT questions and their learners' ability to answer them offered a way out of boredom and glazed eyes, even at the end of a long day. "Zoom fatigue," as it came to be known, eventually set in almost everywhere.

One learner, reflecting upon what he had lost, wrote this: "Sometimes I like it that I can stay at home from school. I can eat at home and sleep later than I could before. But often times I miss my friends, and I can't pay attention to my work. My favorite part about going into school was recess. My friends and I would all eat lunch together and then we would play basketball."

We may have experienced somewhat less of the fatigue than happened elsewhere, but in the end it found us out, even though, for the most part, our learners remained not only faithful to, but even enthusiastic about their appointments. When they were not present, there was usually a good reason.

The tutors rose to the challenge with great ingenuity. A few used rap, listening to it and then writing it, to awaken a dull day, and the results could be good. "I'm playing Friday Night Funkin' with Jack from under my bed" one lyric began; "I've got my favorite shirt on, and it's the color red." Animal books also became popular, especially if the animal was unfamiliar -- buffaloes, for example.

But the first resort was to Raz-Kids books, often to books intended for more advanced readers, which sometimes the learner could read with a little help, and sometimes tutor and learner could read together and then discuss. It is interesting that it was not particularly helpful for the tutor simply to read such books to the learner, though that is a strategy we have used in other times and places, usually with high-interest books that were beyond the learner's reading level.

But here, it often became a good thing in appearance only, no doubt because the Raz-Kids Program, the excellence of which I have often applauded, happily allows for interaction in its practice. So unless the book was high-interest indeed, having the tutor just read it to the learner soon became a bore. The interaction took many forms, from exchanging high and low points in their day (peaks and pits, as tutors and learners put it) as a warm up activity to writing descriptions as such to how to make the perfect PB&J sandwich.

But other books, when they could be found online, were often just as effective, partly because they lay outside of the usual tutorial orbit and were interesting for that reason, partly because the tutors' original FIAT questions seemed to engender conversation more easily, perhaps because they sounded like conversation from the beginning.

One tutor saw, when her learner first joined her online, that the girl was just back from school and tired, so she opted for what thereafter became a favorite book, "I'm the Small One," about the shortest girl in a class, which her learner was, too. This tutor was one of the most able, and used both the Raz-Kids comprehension questions and FIAT questions of her own devising to engage her learner easily, with the result that tiredness gave way to a happy exchange. Another student perceptively saw that her learner's questions indicated that she had never had a history lesson and didn't know what it was. The tutor devised some other readings to speak to that.

Indeed, throughout this year of COVID, FIAT questions have been the life of our party, and the degree to which students have been able to mix them with the Raz-Kids questions, which have the added advantage of providing credits for virtual purchases, have been a fair if unmeasured indicator of progress.

Two tutors were able to resort to online videos. One sang their praises, while the other was more circumspect. But one of the best new strategies, even though not all the tutors used it, was to have guest speakers come in and share a screen with the tutor and learner. The guest speaker was usually another tutor, often one the learner knew already, but if not, at least one who knew the ropes, knew what to say and how, and whose presence quickly put everyone at ease. One student brought in her boyfriend, who is on the sailing team, and who happily explained about sailing boats to the entranced learner. Attentive to our learners' safety as we were, we took care that no strangers appeared in our program.

Situations differed from one guest speaker to another, but what certainly worked best in more than one group was when the presiding tutor carefully presented the promise of a third party to the learner, not only explaining what was to come, but also deciding with the learner what questions they would ask, how they might demonstrate the learner's skills and ability, and what might be a fun activity to do. During one of these sessions, and after a certain amount of pedagogical initiative, the guest speaker suggested that they all draw pictures about the story they had been reading, to show whatever it was in it that made them happy. The best one was the learner's, they all agreed, who showed herself with her tutor and her new friend – the guest speaker – with each one holding up an ice cream cone.

But I must not make the end of the semester sound too easy. During our last few weeks together before the academic year ended, things more or less continued as they had, albeit with a few more bumps along the way: zoom calls intended to begin a tutorial session sometimes went unanswered, and other calls meant to initiate make up sessions found no one at home. But in my last virtual meeting with the tutors at the end of this decidedly difficult academic year, no one regretted that we had carried on. Continuing concern for our learners was palpable, and our sense was that whatever we had accomplished was no small thing. We had carried on as well as circumstances allowed. As for myself, I wondered what was to come, and exactly where next September would find us.

Autumn 2021

And as it happened, we had not long to wait. As May drew to a close, I had again considered, but only for a moment, if we might have reached the end of our virtual program's history; although our arrangements for Georgetown students teaching their young learners in Golden Rule Apartments online might be improved, everything was more or less as it should be, and we would not have to contend with online teaching again for the foreseeable future. But then the pandemic, having first receded, rose up again, this time in a new variant called Delta, and the corner seemed not to have been turned after all. But Georgetown, like most universities, felt itself financially and perhaps in other ways unable to countenance another year of online teaching. Though reasons were never given, the consensus among the colleagues with whom I discussed the matter seemed to suggest the financial necessity of dorm fees and the general advisability of not excluding the students from campus for yet another year, for reasons social, academic, and administrative.

Initially, our plan had been simply to return to pre-pandemic practices, with the Georgetown students visiting the Golden Rule Apartments twice a week, on Tuesday and Thursday, and then meeting with me on campus on Wednesday for our usual seminar. As the Delta variant leapt across the nation, however, such a plan became less feasible. I spoke to some sympathetic nurses and doctors whom I knew, and they confirmed what I had guessed: that the vaccinated could indeed become infected in spite of their vaccinations by "breakthrough infections," as they are called. They could then unknowingly infect an unvaccinated child, like those whom we teach. The obvious solution was the one Bradley and I came to reach. (Bradley had kindly agreed to remain my colleague this semester too, albeit online, since he was now teaching in Florida.) The tutors would continue to instruct online, as they had last year, though there were several who were entirely new to the program, and so required instruction both in Raz-Kids, and in tutoring itself.

For now, however, the real challenge promised to be the learners, not the tutors. They were all back in class, meeting with their friends every day after a year apart, and whether they would be willing to return to their early haunts with tutors seemed problematic. Added to that was the inconvenience, sometimes amounting to a disruption, that I knew we could sometimes bring into our learners' apartment homes, where a two-bedroom apartment could house three or more children. Although it had been easy enough to dispatch one or two off to a reading program in the basement, it was more of an inconvenience for the family as a whole to secure space for a meaningful online tutorial to take place. When I explained what our practice was to be this semester, and the reason for it, to Mr. Foster, our excellent connection at Golden Rule Apartment, he deferred judgment to the parents. As I write, we are still in the process of making and securing assignments, and everything now seems at least to be going as well as we could wish under the circumstances.

Several Days Later...

The parents, to whom our tutors always speak before starting work, have again proved most kind and supportive, and though it will take another week or two before our ducks are in a row, things at this point look well enough. What seems to have been most convincing to parents and learners alike was their experience of last year, and the sense that many of the parents felt that good work was being done with their children at a time and in a way that was unexpected. But there may be more to it than that. Recently, there have been a plethora of newspaper and magazine articles describing "What Our Children Have Lost" during the pandemic. While I cannot contend that our program supplied athletics or field trips or chemistry labs, it certainly supplied a bright and supportive social connection at a time when such things were in short supply. When we began last March, our learners welcomed their tutors warmly, the more so, I suspect, since they were, for the most part, already known by them, and so it constituted an enduring link when many things seemed to be disappearing. So viva our tutors and viva Raz-Kids as well! Thanks to Bradley's good instruction, it looks as though it will flourish this year, too. This semester, however, only one tutor is still with us from last year; I only hope our new tutors will fare as well as their predecessors. But we seem to have a fair wind, and when I last spoke to Mr. Foster, he seemed to me if anything even more encouraging, I hope as a result of having spoken to our learners' parents.

One other seemingly minor issue seems to me important nonetheless, and it has to do with new tutor expectations. Georgetown University, being the sort of place it is, both attracts and produces students who have difficulty, sometimes, in understanding why it is that a sent email or a left message is not responded to promptly. They assume that all with whom they now connect share their attachment to the pen or the keyboard. The process of detachment from such beliefs is usually gradual, but one thing our program teaches is how much we mistakenly assume about others, even those whom we do not know at all. We sometimes learn about ourselves as we do so, and so cross new borders as we go. Experience may keep a dear school, but some will still prefer it to any other – not always without reason. Still, I must not get ahead of myself and assume my conclusions. After all, time will tell. It always has.

October 15

I have not written in this account for three weeks now, though there have been things to report, many having to do with finding out if our learners had moved over the summer, and if they had, whether they were still in our program. We also wondered if we had found learners eager to work with our tutors – a challenge familiar enough from our years at Sursum Corda, when we were twice our present size. Our efforts were complicated by the fact that good Mr. Foster, who had contributed so much to our work during the year of the pandemic, resigned his position in order to return to college, though neither he nor anyone else alerted us to that fact. We thrashed around for a week or so, but in the end we were able to carry on even without his help, and our learners' parents were nothing if not supportive. We were able to locate missing learners and identify new ones, and with, that our program sprang to life again. But as that was going on, I did not feel constrained to detail every difficulty that came our way.

While we were developing the program with new tutors, however, we did not fail to notice that our major strength stood in danger of becoming also our major weakness: distance no longer mattered. Bradley has now taken his M.A. and is teaching in Florida, but has continued tutoring Malcolm, his nine-year-old Golden Rule learner, online. He does so both to become even more expert with online tutoring, and because he remains interested in seeing if our process might have other uses. It may even make it possible for Georgetown students based in Washington DC to teach children living in Louisiana through Georgetown's still developing "Descendants Project," which aims to redress the university's unconscionable sale of 272 slaves to Louisiana slave dealers in 1838.

And of course, such a project might point to other possibilities as well. Worldwide, education is still for the few, not the many, and as years go on, and students move beyond primary school, the disparity only widens. Need this be so? Before the pandemic, to be sure, Zoom had shown a way in which massive online courses could be mobilized with a handful of teachers, but what usually emerged from such teaching was the provision of information and skills, not education in any larger sense, and certainly only a limited investment in other persons or other places, whether as teachers or students, or both. Time will tell, since one property of online teaching is to work against education's innate tendency against difference and favor elitism. But the danger is that this change and others will simply come about piecemeal, without a meaningful attempt at something like a comprehensive review, and that, of course, would be a pity.

These interests have borne in upon us this semester because all of the students tutoring this semester have become interested in the long-term implications of the online teaching we have been doing. Two of the young men in the class are Muslim, one Hindu; all three have proved particularly alert to the ways in which our work might inform education in places where its practice may be uneven, its presence unpredictable. We have discussed, in seminar and out, the ways in which it might be possible to educate students outside of a traditional institutional setting in a way that would not fail to satisfy what we have come to call the "human factor," the ability of persons to interact and respond to each other and to ideas and explanations in an academic environment, without which education hardly exists at all.

The danger with virtual learning, of course, is that the education it produces could thus more easily become a plaything of the state, a circumstance which many a dictator would hasten to embrace, as some have sought to do already. But without dismissing this real concern, experience suggests that there is a power in education that, rough-hew it as we will, will not disappear, no matter how tyrants might fight or try to manipulate it. And as everyone has only recently grasped, Zoom has made things possible that were not before, and we have only just begun to test its reach. Its future may indeed seem to be everywhere, but the physical, legal, diplomatic, and cultural barriers that currently constrain its operation are not illusions, and will not easily be put aside. As for us, standing where we are and working as we do, we can only address gently, and with what understanding we discover, the cultural and pedagogical challenges implicit in our work.

Programs like ours must thus go carefully. One of the most perceptive lines in Henry David Thoreau's *Walden* comes when he is discussing what we must reckon with today as well: not only the usefulness of any new technology, but also its dangers. For Thoreau, that was the startlingly new world of railways, not Zoom or Raz-Kids, but the effects do not much differ. Like us, Thoreau saluted the attractive new world the railway brought with it, the making of a new world market, speeding goods to the consumer, even redefining, once again, the power of time. But he understood as well that technology does not only follow, it also leads, and there is no man so powerful as to deny it. No farmer sends his produce to market by horse and wagon anymore, and for faster rides you'll need an iron horse; but if you need leisure time, you'd better plan it carefully, and count the hours.

Technology must be investigated, that's for sure, not taken for granted, and that is nowhere more true than it is in education. One result of our discussion last night in seminar of the evident international implications and the apparent new openings that online teaching offers is that in the future I mean to add more poetry to our curriculum. Perhaps we could start with one who was a great favorite in the Sursum Corda program: Langston Hughes. His poems were attractive to tutor and learner alike, as much for their rhythm and their humor as for their occasionally ignored content, which was sometimes not appropriate for our learners.

"Midnight Raffle" was one such, and though the object of the quest was rarely dwelt upon, there may still be among our former learners those who, without remembering its source, can still recall some of its proto-rap lyrics: "I lost my nickel. / I lost my time. / I got back home / Without a dime." But we would sometimes pair Langston Hughes, unlikely though it may sound, with Robert Frost, whose "Stopping by Woods on a Snowy Evening" became a favorite of tutor and learner alike, particularly when read by the tutor dramatically, with a ghost-like voice to evoke the silence of landscape, "the darkest evening of the year."

It is difficult for two people to read poetry together aloud, whether virtually or face-to- face, without also engaging with each other. Raz-Kids may have somewhat constrained our program from plunging deeply into poetry, but our tutors, as the British say, need try their arm at many things if they are to engage with our learners in the potentially deadening world of online education. These are early days yet for virtual learning, and we must not lose heart. As Dr. Johnson says, "What good is a baby?"

22 October

Bradley has been in Washington this week, thanks to a dispensation from the school in which he is now teaching, and came to speak to our seminar last night. His topic was Georgetown's "Descendants Project," an effort of the university that seeks to address the university's sale of 272 slaves to slave dealers from Louisiana in 1838. It figured prominently in one episode of Henry Lewis Gates, Jr.'s TV series "Finding Your Roots," produced by Public Broadcasting in 2020, and is echoed as well in the exhibition on slavery in the Smithsonian Museum of African-American History and Culture in Washington, DC. But the issue has become increasingly complicated, since over the years Georgetown, like most older universities, "owned" far more than 272 slaves – the number must run into the thousands – and there are said to be large numbers of descendants now living not only in Louisiana, but also throughout Maryland, in St. Louis, Missouri, and elsewhere. The effort is now being called Georgetown's "Reconciliation Effort," so as to take the larger circumstances into account.

At the suggestion of a woman with whom Bradley met some years ago during a Georgetown-sponsored trip to the descendants' community in Marigouin, Louisiana, the university is considering offering an online tutoring program with Georgetown undergraduates to the children there. The presentation echoed last week's discussion, when we had mooted among ourselves the implications of the work we have been doing, and concluded that instruction over distance was one of the more obvious.

Bradley's talk, which had noted carefully how important it was to consult with and accept direction from those whom you hope to serve, occasioned a thoughtful discussion among the students, with one woman adding perceptively that such programs could also inform the current discourse concerning disability. But that, in turn, raised the question of the relationship that develops between tutor and learner, and Bradley registered the necessity, in more formal teaching at any rate, of a degree of distance between teacher and student in order for the teaching to succeed. We agreed, I think, that although "friendship" is not at all the right word by which to describe the relationship that exists between tutor and learner, a morsel of it is by no means out of place in one-on-one online teaching, which otherwise can become a grind, remorseless for tutor or learner alike. This seems a minor point, someone said, but really it isn't. This became clear when Bradley talked about his work with his excellent learner Malcolm, now in the third grade, and noted how a simple thing like a facial expression could give new energy to their work, since by now they know each other rather well. But their tutorial is watched over as well by Malcolm's mother, who, like others elsewhere, keeps an eye on things.

Thus, their relationship, delimited by distance, is further constrained by others in the apartment. Virtual learning is rarely undertaken alone.

November

And now November has come upon us, and in this class, as in most, the die has been cast, and the end is in sight. In seminar last week we were discussing Toni Morrison's *Beloved*, the novel which, though not respected as it should have been at publication, rose up to lead the way to the author's much deserved Nobel Prize.

What we were attempting was not so much to analyze or decode the work itself, as to consider what use, what relevance, it had for our endeavors. Although, to tell the truth, not every student had read every word, we began by agreeing that it certainly set in stone the proposition that the effects of slavery are still with us, and that we are all suffering from them, black and white, yellow, red, and brown, and everyone who lives in this land of ours. But the point is not to wallow in those effects, but to address them meaningfully and as best we can.

The bloody and quite awful event that is central to *Beloved* gains in credibility from its actually having happened, and so does the book, both by that event and by having been set in post-bellum Ohio, which is Everywhere; its narrative is very far from over.

But we wondered too, at least those of us who had gotten that far, about its ending. Beloved the ghost was gone, but courageous and now hopeful Denver seemed ready to take part in life again, mostly urged on by her Black neighbors, but encouraged by other friends as well, some of them White. We tried not to make too much of this circumstance, of course, but found it interesting, and thought it mattered. Many of the Whites in the book are unmistakably dreadful, though there are a few exceptions. And these exceptions, I suppose, are our allies, or we are theirs, alert to the unspeakable harm that slavery has done, by the unfairness it continues to unleash, and by the gaps among us all that matter still. Our one step here at Golden Rule may help bring us to that day that is to come, a day we dare to hope for and predict. We join our voice to others' gone before, and find our silence and our song in doing so.

12 December

We had two final seminars to go, after the one in which we grappled with *Beloved*, one in which my friend Officer Darrin Bates of the MPD visited to tell the class about growing up in and around Sursum Corda, an area that embraced Golden Rule Apartments as well, and another in which we revisited our final weeks, and got our ducks in a row for going as a group to Golden Rule and meeting the children we have been teaching all semester. I wasn't sure how Officer Bates' visit would go. He had visited our seminar in the past, when tutors and learners knew each other well from their twice-weekly tutorials, but this time they had never actually met, nor had the tutors any idea at all about the area in which their learners live. When he came, he sounded themes he had introduced before – about the difference between day and night in and around Sursum Corda itself, about the effects of growing up in a place and time when drugs and violence were daily visitors, about what it was like to meet Georgetown students, so green in one way, so interesting in another -- but the tutors were fascinated by what he had to say, listened attentively, asked good and, it seemed to me, quite perceptive questions, and subsequently referred quite accurately to what he had said in their course papers.

Finally, in our last seminar together, we prepared to visit those whom we had come to know. But before we did so, we summarized our last few weeks together. Thanksgiving had taken a toll, and learners – not tutors – had cancelled meetings in favor of family gatherings with turkey, but even so, good will abounded. And this good note as well: poetry has begun to take root. What I had hoped for – that poetry might in some way mitigate the impersonal distance that online learning somehow carries with it -- has been embraced by two – perhaps three – of the tutors, and wonderful results were reported from having read together and discussed Maya Angelou's fine poem "Life Doesn't Frighten Me," and one or two others. It was a great way to end the semester, one tutor thought.

But even so, the difficulties this semester posed were greater than I had expected, perhaps even greater than those of the previous year, in which tutor and learner were already acquainted when the lockdown began, and the challenge was to decide how to proceed, a challenge greatly assisted by Raz-Kids. This time, after all, we had to begin from the beginning, navigating both meeting for the first time and also establishing a sense of syllabus, both more or less at the same time. In some cases the learners led their tutors into battle. For these reasons, and no doubt for others too, the December visit, which began about 4pm and was held outdoors, went as well as anyone could have wished. The children, shy at first, responded to their smart tutors' gentle questions, and also to the pizza when it came. It was excellent to see Fred Hawkins there, and we talked together, me a little critically, about Paolo Freire and then about our program's hopes for the future. The party, for so we called it, lasted a little over an hour, ending about 5:20, when it was too dark to play. Afterward the tutors sang their pleasure in the meeting, and promised to return again come spring, but also to continue work online. At that moment it seemed the thing to say, though I have no doubt they meant it, and agreed. But later, trying to think through what I had seen, I began to think there was a better way. The pandemic taught us the art of online tutoring – viva Raz-Kids, but viva the tutors too. And for the tutors, online tutoring is a convenience, that's for sure. They can arrange a time that fits in with their active, busy lives, and end a few minutes early if they must, or go on a little longer, if things are going well. But if that party – and thirty years of face-to-face tutoring at Sursum Corda, three at Golden Rule, that had come before -- meant anything, it meant that these is no substitute for en-counter. Tutor and learners were alike surprised that their virtual counterparts were large, had limbs that moved, and could eat (pizza) and drink (fruit juice) to prove they were not ghosts who lived only on a small screen. What we need to consider now is the possibility and usefulness of a hybrid program, one in which tutors and learners would visit once weekly – or once every two weeks? -- face-to-face, and once or twice or three times a fortnight online, according to his or her ability or need. It would thus be possible to do more in less space and time, and perhaps engage more tutors and learners for longer, depending upon their mutual esteem. If the last twenty months have taught us anything, it is that there is more, not less, need for the work we do. The tutors' good energy has matched and often enkindled their learners', and together they have made a bright way in a sad time. But these are early days for those of us who have, thus far, survived the perilous seas of the pandemic, and though we have no golden bough to ensure our passage, a return to the upper air again is now our task, our work, our joy.

Photo Gallery

CPSIA information can be obtained
at www.ICGtesting.com
Printed in the USA
JSHW051759100922
30264JS00003B/5

9 798985 221435